THE ULTIMATE BETRAYAL

Dealing with the Increasing Senior
Financial Abuse, the Loss of Wealth, and
the Need for Setting Boundaries

A Concept

Anne McGowan

CEO of Protecting Seniors Wealth

Archway Publishing books may be ordered
through booksellers or by contacting:

Archway Publishing
1663 Liberty Drive
Bloomington, IN 47403
www.archwaypublishing.com
1 (888) 242-5904

ISBN: 978-1-4808-3282-4 (sc)
ISBN: 978-1-4808-3284-8 (hc)
ISBN: 978-1-4808-3283-1 (e)

Library of Congress Control Number: 2016909712

Print information available on the last page.

Archway Publishing rev. date: 07/29/2016

CONTENTS

Author's Note.. ix

1 | There's a Triple-Whammy Effect 1
They Manipulate It on the Sly 1

2 | It's Reaching Epidemic Proportions.................................. 9
It Changed the Course of My Life!.. 9

3 | Elder Security Becomes More Relevant........................ 16
Helping Parents Was My Gift to Them 16

4 | The Dilemma in Relation to Assessment........................ 24
When Older Parents Seem Upset.. 24

5 | The Complications of Stepping In 34
The Process toward a Hearing 34

6 | Being a Voice for the Elders 43
Our Seniors Should Be Valued... 43

7 | An Important Overview 52
Where Does the Family Wealth Go? 52

8 | The Makings of the Guide... 61
The Result of Everyone's Stories....................................... 61

9 | The Truth of the Matter, and How It Goes Unnoticed 71
A Concept called Inheritance Impatience 71

10 | It's Their Money, and It's Their Whole Wealth......................84
Having Money Should Be a Good Thing.......................................84

11 | Other Insights about the Gray Area..95
The Idea of a Register 95

12 | Maintaining Seniors' Wealth and Protecting Their
          Whole Wealth.. 103
It's Time We All Say No! 103

Acknowledgments... 119
About the Author 121
About Protecting Seniors Wealth and the Benefit of
          Training Workshops.. 125
Other Book.. 127
Parkinson's Disease 129
References for this Book.. 131
For Additional Information 133

For the elder senior citizens throughout the world who have worked all their lives and dedicated that work to raising their families and being good citizens. Thanks to their efforts, contributions, and endeavors, they have created a world of which we can all be proud.

For all the dedicated lawyers worldwide who work tirelessly in the area of elder law to help to protect our elder seniors.

And in memory of my father, William John McGowan (1932–2011).

> Our lives begin to end the day we become silent about things that matter.
> —Martin Luther King

Author's Note

If someone had said to me six years ago that I'd be publishing a book on this subject, I would not have believed it. As I began writing, a wonderful woman who had experienced this type of situation mentioned the quote in chapter 1. I thank her for her honesty, and she put a name to it. Although it sounds harsh, that's what it is: abuse of the elderly for their money. Unfortunately, it's far more common than we think.

Some of you are already forming the opinion that this won't happen to you, your family, or someone you know. I have to confess that I didn't know it happened either—or at least not to the extent it does. Yes, the statistics are alarming, and the rate at which it occurs is increasing. Considering we have an aging population who controls a larger portion of the wealth in the world, chances are it will happen to a lot more elders. It is for these reasons that I sincerely encourage you to become informed and be aware of the pitfalls. Stop for a moment, and take some time to consider whether changes should be made—and how.

Setting some boundaries earlier, rather than when it becomes too late to prevent elder financial abuse, is far easier and creates less heartache for older citizens and their loved ones. This harsh form of deceit may not occur at all to an elder to whom you're close. You may have a beautiful supportive family and a trustworthy network of people around you, and that's wonderful. Taking preventative steps is far easier than trying to deal with the loss of loved ones' dignity, the loss of their money to support the way of life they've chosen, and (eventually) the loss of people's inheritances and even happiness. Sadly, the more I found out as I was compelled to look into the issue and investigate this topic, the more shocked I became at the inhumanity of humanity.

Today, after many years, I'm choosing to face reality: this occurs, and it's much more widespread than we realize. It's not spoken of, because it's embarrassing, it hurts those who have been taken advantage of, and it upsets people hearing about it. However, I am now strongly of the view that if I can help make things better for others so that they don't have to experience the same indignity of the ultimate betrayal, I will feel as though I've done something constructive. If I can help to prevent this from happening to other elder people, then at least something good will come out of a very sad and disappointing form of human behavior that's quite prevalent in our society.

If, along the way, we can help to create more awareness and possibly improve something in the legal structure to better protect elders, these initiatives could not only help the legal profession do their work but would be a very good outcome indeed if it helped to minimize elder wealth abuse. It's about protecting the elders—their well-being, their wealth, and their right to live as they choose, make their own choices, and bequeath inheritance as they see fit. They have the right to live out their days as they wish to do so, in comfort, and to fully enjoy their lives. Many have spent their lives working on their wealth to do just that—not to have someone come along and take it. How people take it is covered in detail in this book. As I was compelled to delve into the subject, I was told many, many stories about the process.

I hope this work will create more awareness, educate people, help to change things, and possibly prevent this from occurring to lovely older people who should instead be valued. The content is also about offering some ideas that go somewhat toward helping to heal those who have experienced this firsthand and were adversely affected by this low behavior. The people who carry out this form of elder abuse can be manipulative and ruthless. It can leave the innocent people affected feeling quite devastated, helpless, and often fearful.

This book is not just about protecting your wealth. It has the potential to be used as a basic conceptual framework in order to change things, improve systems, and minimize the risks for our senior citizens as they age. As part of that, it's also about how to create your "whole wealth"—the feeling of truly being happy, how to enjoy it, and how to have a really good life. There are also useful ideas that may assist you if you're helping to care for elders.

The concept exposed in this book is about looking to create awareness and improve or change this issue for the better now—not putting it in the "too hard" basket and certainly not hiding from it because it's not a nice subject or is upsetting. For some, it's too embarrassing or demoralizing—the fact that it even happened in your family or to an older person dear to you. There are many things people can do to improve the protection of our elders, both now and as we progress. Perhaps we could consider embracing this concept and embarking on a campaign where we consider what is possible in order to help us tackle this issue head-on and ultimately improve this predicament while we can. After all, when you think about it, we will all be elders ourselves one day.

1

There's a Triple-Whammy Effect

They Manipulate It on the Sly

Say not you know another entirely, till you have divided an inheritance with him.

—Johann Kasper Lavatar

Why on earth am I writing about elder financial abuse, when elder people may not even read it? This book will most likely be read by middle-aged people who are assisting in giving care for elders in their personal lives or chosen professions. I most certainly hope it will be read by the people in our world who are responsible for ensuring the law is carried out, and by the people who can effectively adjust or change something in the structure of our legal systems. The people I'm referring to are the ones involved in our legal systems, plus politicians and those in key positions in our governments.

This is also about your whole wealth. For a couple of very good reasons that will become obvious as we take a closer look at what is happening, abuse of the elderly in whatever form, in order to access their assets, is not a pleasant subject, and unfortunately it is widespread. Perhaps it's time we collectively do something about it. Isn't it time we find our voices, speak up, and take action?

In doing so, our actions will say, "No, this is no longer going to be allowed or overlooked in our society!"

Perhaps you might find yourself saying, "I'm going to see what I can do about this because I don't want to endure this when I get older." Believe me when I say that this is certainly something you will not want your children to experience. The effects of elder wealth abuse have the potential to break up families and devastate innocent people. Knowing what I now know about how it happens and what perpetrators do to the elders to access their money, it's highly likely you will want to avoid your children having to be involved if this happens to a grandfather or grandmother whom they dearly love. It's heartbreaking for children at such a young age, it is horrible for elders, and it will affect you too if it occurs in your family.

When you know more about this, you will not want your children to experience it firsthand when they grow older themselves. By now you may have some questions, and just as I did, you might find yourself asking, "There must be something that can be done. How do we actually do that?" There's no denying that the thought of this happening to our own family members or elderly people we know is awful and distressing. It's not only these lovely elderly people who have their choices taken from them—including their money, houses, happiness, self-esteem, and dignity. It happens to us too. Yes, us!

Knowing what may be done or has been done to these frail older people weighs very heavily on you—even more so if it actually happens. The knowledge of an elderly person you love being abused can weigh so heavily on you that it drains your sense of well-being. Experiencing it can significantly drag down the level of a person's happiness and wellness. The other factor—and it's a highly common outcome—is that if this form of wealth abuse is occurring, one can lose one's inheritance in the process. Many people do. If you know where to look, the statistics are quite alarming, and yet it's not being spoken about often enough to make a difference.

This fact didn't even occur to me, until the reality of the whole scenario hit me like a ton of bricks. The people who deliberately embark on a scheme to take an older person's money or assets also takes someone's inheritance. The consequence is a loss of wealth and support to live, as well as much heartache, especially for the elders who've been victimized. One of the first lawyers I spoke with regarding this matter considered all the details, and he inferred people often find out too late. I'll always remember his remark: "Then they've already done it, Anne." In many cases it's been carried out so cunningly that no one knows, or the family members are not aware of what is really happening, with the exception of possibly the elder person. In many cases people find out all too late, and the deed is already done! In these cases, it may be difficult to prove the theft or take action.

I sat there in that meeting, stunned for a moment while digesting what the lawyer had implied. I looked at him incredulously to see whether he was being earnest, and I said, "Do you mean to tell me that some people can do this?" Initially I thought he was simply being complacent. Unfortunately, upon looking back after hearing all the stories I have been told over the last six years, I think he was being up-front and matter-of-fact with us. At that time he was working on cases of elder financial abuse, and many lawyers I've conferred with since have mentioned how they are working on such cases. I still vividly recall how it hit me when that lawyer said something about how the law doesn't protect the elderly.

Many other people have made the same comment since then. There is in fact a law in place to deal with this, and it's called undue influence. This is not my area of expertise, but it does look like an appropriate law that should help to protect elders.

The problem seems to lie somewhere between the difficulties of being able to prove any wrongdoing, to having someone who is informed assisting them, to obtaining the evidence required (medical or otherwise). To make matters more complicated, the elders can either be reluctant to take action because they're so upset about it or be unable to for a number of reasons. Those quite alarming reasons will be explained in more detail as we take a broader look at this issue.

When I began to look further into the aspects of elder financial abuse, and I met with the lawyer I mentioned earlier, one of the things he spoke of was how, in order to assist his legal work, he studied psychology. He was generalizing, of course, but he spoke of the behavior of people with childhood-abuse backgrounds in relation to how they might behave if subjected to wealth abuse. If I understood him correctly, he basically said that often elders will be submissive, or perhaps they will say one thing to one person and another to someone else, or they'll simply go along with what they're being told to do. People who have experienced abuse may react differently. It's a complicated area, and I assume not everyone will react in the same way, but taking this into consideration helps us begin to understand just how easily elders can be taken advantage of.

While further looking into aspects of elder wealth abuse, I learned of some other key information with respect to our elders and what can occur as they age. This information perhaps could be important to know in order to help us understand what can take place. The general comments were based on medical research and also highlight the need to prepare for being an elder some years before one reaches that stage. I found this information interesting because it explained how some elders may begin to experience the onset of age-related problems, making it more difficult for them to keep track of their finances. These elders could still manage to manage other aspects of their lives quite normally. I'm not an expert, but it does explain how so many elders are financially taken advantage of. It emphasizes why they sometimes need someone they can trust to help with their finances. In some cases, their capacity may diminish to a certain extent in this regard, and they may find it difficult to effectively head off the perpetrators, who are looking to take advantage of them.

In the cases where the elders who may have had an abusive background are concerned, this fact, coupled with any possible onset of advanced aging difficulties, leaves them without the defenses needed to stand up to the cunning operators. To leave out this aspect would mean leaving out crucial key information that would help people understand the difficulties of stepping in, and why the perpetrators manage to do it. It also highlights the importance of how, in some cases, the need to consider whether an assessment would be worthwhile. It may even play an important role in protecting them.

Committing the act of wealth abuse is something I would never contemplate doing to someone, so I didn't imagine it would happen as much as it does. When I first stumbled across this issue and grappled with just how big a deal it is, my head reeled for a while. In leading my life, I always thought I would lead by example and do the right thing, and others would treat people with the same respect. But they certainly do not.

That is the final insult following elder financial abuse for their money: it has a triple-whammy effect. First, the elders are subjected to being manipulated or abused. Second, they lose their wealth, their means to support themselves; they not only are devastated but experience a loss of dignity, and they become fearful. Third, they lose the inheritance they had planned to leave their loved ones. That third aspect is usually very important to elders, and it's taken away from them.

In addition, the perpetrators can carry out an aggressive and lengthy campaign aimed directly at getting the decent people caring for the elders out of the way. The tactics they use can often be comprised of ongoing defamatory remarks, insults, incorrect accusations or blatant lies, abusive messages, and more. These sly acts are carried out to get the decent people out of the way so that the perpetrators can access the elders' wealth. Afterward, the final insult is the realization that someone's inheritance is taken as well. However, the worst part is the abuse of an elder person and that person's basic rights.

The reality is that in many cases, perpetrators not only manage to commit the ultimate betrayal against elders but take people's inheritances. An inheritance is something that means a lot to some people—not because of the amount of money, but because it is meant to be a gift that parents leave their loved ones. Just as my husband and I will proudly leave something for our daughter, so will most parents leave an inheritance for their children if they can, and they will certainly hope the children rightfully get it.

I know both my parents and my husband's parents had stated that in their wills. They had been adamant, clear, and certain about it for the last twenty plus years of their lives. In fact, both our parents had drawn up their wills at least fifteen to twenty years before the onset of any health problems. It doesn't seem right that some corrupt person can come along and abuse the elderly to change their wills or take their money. In some situations, financial abuse is carried out by more than one person—and as unbelievable as it sounds, they actually encourage each other. The prospect of getting the money becomes a priority and turns into a cunning scheme of manipulation.

The occurrence of financial abuse of the elderly for money or assets could happen to you too. According to the statistics, there is a high chance the perpetrator could be a family member. In addition, although we know and appreciate that there are mostly highly professional people who help us care for elders, there are a few people who manipulate and take advantage of the elders.

Here's one example. An elderly parent or person suddenly finds a new friend, or someone posing as a financial advisor or carer. At some point, you may get a sense that something isn't right. If you do, follow your instincts and take a closer look. Be informed and be prepared. I sincerely wish I had known about the extent of all this wealth abuse much earlier. Perhaps those of us with some sense of respect, responsibility, and knowledge should assist and shine a light on this issue.

It did occur to me that if people were more aware, prepared, assertive, and confident, then they could then confidently threaten the perpetrators with legal action. Knowledge makes it easier to effectively step in and stop it. If the predators plotting to do this knew actions can and will be taken, it may stop them from proceeding, or it might delay their actions for a while until something can legally be done to protect the elders involved. Financial fraud is also elder abuse, plain and simple.

However, it may not deter them. The sad thing is elders usually know when they've been swindled. In most cases, elders will know at some point what the scammers are up to. Elder people are not silly; often they are just simply not strong enough to fend them off. The perpetrators are quite relentless; for them, stopping halfway through a scam could mean they'd be exposed. Perhaps that's why they carry out doing this so relentlessly and ruthlessly. They are intent on getting the money, and that is what this is about. They don't seem to stop to consider or care whether they ruin someone's reputation in the process—or even worse, devastate an elder person.

I now realize, and frequently have to remind myself, that the people who plan to do this may present themselves very well, wearing decent clothes and speaking as if they care. But they actually do plan this attack; they consider the timing, deliberately take a course of action, and plan to get away with it. They're chasing the money or the perceived power it might bring, and they will not care whether they hurt you or others who stand in their way, including the elders. Sometimes it's manipulated so cunningly, like a fox raiding a chicken coop at night, and no one realizes until sometime later, after it's done!

Other times, especially if there's more than one person involved, and you're the good person who will obviously block any of this activity, they will attempt to run over you like a bowling ball knocks down pins, using their well-thought-out tactics. What was perhaps once a thought to access an elder's money can become a plan, and if they continue it, it becomes an obsession. Look out if you're the innocent one standing in the way, because they will tell convincing lies if they need to.

By all accounts, perpetrators often do whatever they can to discredit you, taint your good reputation, and cast wrongful dispersions on your good character. They may also pretend they were the ones who were wronged. In fact, this is how they operate, flying under the radar and going undetected. They twist the truth, lying to such an extent that you can understand why some people think they can't possibly be lying. Surely no one would lie that deliberately or that well, so perhaps the accusations are believable. They may even infer it's always someone else's fault— and they possibly blame it all on you. It's far from the truth, but it's a smoke screen to hide what they're actually doing.

2

It's Reaching Epidemic Proportions

It Changed the Course of My Life!

Shortly after uncovering all of this unnerving information related to elder financial abuse, it began strongly affecting me. Something stirred within me as I came across more and more information, with more people telling me their stories. It's been about four years (the last two were more on a full-time basis) of searching on the Internet, having conversations with people about their experiences, and participating in discussions with professionals ranging from lawyers, accountants, investment advisors, carers or caregivers, real estate agents, and bank staff, as well as numerous organizations. Then I prepared a practical guide for publication. Now, writing about it seems the best way to communicate how this issue is such a growing concern, and to reach as many people as possible.

We're not just talking about hundreds or thousands of elders being affected by financial abuse. It's more like millions throughout the world. This is not a small issue by any means. In fact, most people I speak with these days have either had a firsthand experience or know of someone who has. The many people I have held conversations with regarding their stories spoke damningly about it, when describing their encounters with elder wealth abuse. The topic has changed the course of my life.

As a result, there's no doubt in my mind, after much investigation into the extent of the ultimate betrayal, that elder security will become more and more relevant in the years to come as the population ages. In most countries seniors hold the largest percentage of the wealth. This, along with the fact that many elder seniors may develop age-related health difficulties, makes them an easy target for greedy operators. Before a series of events compelled me to look into this, there were many times when I would reflect back on better times, when life was comparatively quite good. I thought about when I didn't know the extent of what was happening to a large proportion of our elders. Back then I was blissfully unaware, and we were busy conducting our own lives, quite naive at that time about what was happening to so many senior citizens. At Christmas we would gather at my parents' house to celebrate and enjoy a meal together. We celebrated special occasions such as birthdays and anniversaries, and we always kept up to date with the latest developments. But never did I hear about anyone speaking out or speaking up about elder financial abuse.

On my father's side of the family, when I recently looked into the family tree, I found out we were of Irish decent and came from an interesting family. Many of them were people of commerce. Some held high positions in banking, some ran their own businesses, and some operated a small theatre company that apparently entertained the royal children. Generally they did well for themselves. It might explain my interest in business, communication, writing, and the production of good work, including design.

I often think back on those days of innocently going about making our lives. Our lives were full, and we were always busy. I had numerous projects on the go, worked long hours, and sometimes renovated a house. When I met my husband, we bought a lovely rural property, and then I was invited to teach business subjects and coordinate classes at the local colleges. After enjoying our new rural lifestyle for a while, the highlight of our lives arrived when our beautiful daughter was born.

Life continued to be quite busy, we were involved in our community, and we were happy. John, my husband, was a volunteer in two local community organizations. When it became obvious our daughter was very social, I became conscious of participating in numerous activities with her so that she felt supported and her needs were met. We attended two playgroups, swimming lessons, weekly storytelling time at the local library, children's concerts, and dance lessons. It truly was a beautiful time in our lives, and we met a lot of good people and made many friends along the way. We were fortunate in that we could afford to do this. The town we lived in was a good country town with good people, and as a result we felt part of a community and were comfortable with our lives.

We understood the importance of being social, and our daughter had opportunities to mix with a variety of people and develop a wide range of skills. During my own childhood, there was not a lot of socializing or participating in extracurricular activities, possibly because my parents couldn't afford it. The local school functions were our social events. Things were tight financially for my parents back then, as they were for many families. I accepted that, even at such a young age, and it was quite all right with me. I had parents who loved me, we had horses and other animals on a small farm, and that was a very nice way to spend my childhood. I do remember one special treat with my mother while I was still very young. We went to Manly Beach, and Dad caught the ferry into the city of Sydney, because he had some business matters to attend to. Mum bought chocolate éclairs from the baker's shop, and it was such a lovely day out.

Life was simpler back then. Those days were quite different to my adult life. Come to think of it, in my adult life I was always involved in studies or a course of some kind, or reading and learning about something of interest. But for me as a mother and a wife, family came first! My parents were very much a part of that family, as were my husband's parents. Even though I still enjoyed being productive and gaining knowledge, it was more whenever there was time. Raising a child and leading a good life as a family unit can be very busy; it passes by quickly, but it is truly a fabulous experience. I still have wonderful memories of reading all these fabulous stories to our daughter. We still laugh about some of those tales told in the children's books, even today. It's a marvelous way to share some enjoyment with your child or children.

Back then, I always thought people would learn discernment at some point; they'd grow up, grow older, get wiser, and become mature. Most good people do so. However, it has become apparent to me that some people simply don't—they decide to take a much different path. Some people can regress, or they go down the wrong path. Perhaps they have not very good influences in their lives, and they mix with bad crowds. Some people are aggressors who impose their will on other weaker people, and some are control freaks whose actions are not conducted in pleasant ways.

Choosing to better myself came naturally to me back then. I kept improving my life and tried to be a good person. As we get older and learn how to make good choices, we can steer away from the not decent people. We can learn to recognize and avoid the people who try to dominate us or take advantage of our good nature, or who simply attempt to take away power and make others feel less than the good people they are. But for some people, especially as they become elders, it can become more difficult to keep these particular types of people out of their lives.

Many years ago, I returned from a rather extended business stay in New Zealand, which I loved. I was in my early thirties at the time and had been working overseas for several years. However, I do remember how it felt so good to come home and visit my parents. It was then that I decided to move back. Everything was going so well in Auckland, and I loved it there, but I thought if I didn't move back, I would probably stay there. My parents were getting older, and it was obvious they would need help at some stage. It was at that time I realized just how important family was to me, and I held the view that family should be supportive of each other. I always try to do that, even with a busy personal life and work schedule.

Leading up to this, I'd been a busy executive, running my own business and consulting to well-known companies. It was hard work with long hours, but it was very enjoyable at the same time. I was fortunate in that I worked with very professional, decent, genuine, caring people. We all worked hard and kept long hours. We carried out the work day to day in an educated way, we were well mannered, and it seemed almost effortless to achieve some of the amazing things we did. All our projects worked out very well, and we were riding the wave of being successful in our lives.

During those days, most of the time I wore business suits and attended lunch meetings and many functions with some highly respected people involved in business, the media, and the government. My business flourished, and it was a very good time in my life. I have learned over the years to trust my instincts and enjoy the company of decent people. I also learned if I get a bad feeling about people or a particular group of people, I do not trust them and steer away from them. Life's too short to have others be negligent and ruin the good things happening in my life. These people who carry out the ultimate betrayal are definitely not to be trusted. If they succeed at carrying out their sly plans, there's no coming back from that, because they actually do ruin people's lives, sometimes permanently.

I used to ask myself, "Why do I do reasonably well?" I think it was because of the way I functioned: by focusing on the outcomes and generally treating people, situations, and lives with respect. Admittedly, I've noticed that not everyone seems to function in this way, especially in recent years. Most people are decent and lead good lives. Sadly, there are some people, who don't seem to make good choices. In fact, they make very poor choices, and some of them are corrupt.

Many people have some difficulties to deal with their lives. Most of us can relate to that, however we all have a choice, and we don't have to make bad choices. I know money difficulties can be a much bigger issue for some, but people don't have to choose to abuse the elderly for money. Instead, they can go elsewhere and learn how to earn their own money and create their own wealth. Scammers have no right doing what they do to some elder people. Our elders should not have to endure ongoing manipulation, emotional or verbal abuse, and the erosion of their self-esteem and identities. They should be able to feel safe and happy in the knowledge that they have led good lives and are secure in their later years.

Those people looking to get their hands on an elder's money should be looking at legal ways to make their own money. There's plenty of help out there for people to build their own wealth in an honest way. There are many courses offered privately, and some are offered by the government to assist the unemployed. I know this from firsthand experience, when I taught various adult business studies at colleges. One of the departments in which I was asked to teach introduced courses to help people train in a new skill, obtain a job, and get back into the workforce. As part of those courses, we would liaise with prospective employees to assist look for employment. The courses had good outcomes with a high number of people being successfully employed.

However, there's a bizarre twist in the issue of senior wealth abuse. It's not just the people who are having money problems who commit the ultimate betrayal against the elderly. People who already have wealth are the perpetrators as well. They will go to great lengths to distort and misrepresent the truth, to persuade and swindle elders in order to grow their own wealth. When you start to see the figures indicating the extent of this atrocity, it's outrageously high. There are many millions of elders, and the figures indicate it's at least in the millions who are losing billions of dollars to this growing epidemic.

3

Elder Security Becomes More Relevant

Helping Parents Was My Gift to Them

You gave me your time,
the most thoughtful gift of all.
—Dan Zadra

It was over twenty years ago when I relocated from Auckland, New Zealand, and settled back into life in Sydney. It wasn't too long afterward that I started helping my parents. They asked me to assist them with their affairs, and we put a lot of time and effort into financially setting up my parents quite well. They were ready to downsize and retire. Up until then, they were perfectly capable and managed their own lives. For my parents, it was when it became time to move and plan for their later years that they enjoyed some assistance. They wanted someone else involved to some extent whom they trusted to help them when needed. They still made their own decisions, but they felt reassured in working with someone who merely assisted, by facilitating what they decided to do.

When we helped my parents move, this was also a time when they became happier and enjoyed a good life full of activity, with financial freedom for many years. It was a time when my parents actually chose to improve their health and be involved in projects and different forms of socializing, and they enjoyed it all very much. They could afford to do it and felt very comfortable. Life was busy and productive. Dad played tennis and made some like-minded friends who were very decent people. Once a week, my mother made the trip to Sydney to see her counselor. Dad would drive her, and he didn't mind because they were both in quite good health. It seemed to help my mother a lot. It was a form of socializing for her, and as a result she participated more in life. It was the happiest I'd seen her in a long time. In fact, I don't think I'd ever seen her quite so happy.

For my parents, having some extra money to do the things they wanted to do in life made all the difference in the world. By this time, they didn't have any dependants living with them, and they led their own lives. Perhaps for the first time in their lives together, they were able to have and do what they wanted from day to day. It made a huge difference for my parents, and it was then I understood why they called it financial freedom. They didn't throw away their money. They still lived quite conservatively because that's the type of people they were, but they had more than enough, so they didn't have to worry about money.

I'd been helping my parents since they'd decided to sell their acreage property and downsize. That property had become too much work for them and was rather run down. They were always trying to make ends meet financially. It wasn't really enjoyable to them anymore, and it was obvious they'd lost enthusiasm for their lives. At first I helped them with their financial and property arrangements, seeking good professional advice and assistance for various matters. We knew people in the area, and it flowed along quite well.

However, as my parents aged, there were health issues that arose. As a result, Dad was finding the drive to Sydney once a week difficult to manage, and so he asked that my mother have her appointments over the phone instead. She didn't take this very well at first and didn't understand that it was beginning to drain my father. At the time I lived over an hour away with a young child. Rather than find another counselor locally, my mother and her current counselor came up with the idea that my mother could call her anytime. I think perhaps my mother also thought she'd had enough of "talking about it." She'd had enough of going over the issues stemming from her childhood, and she simply wanted to relax and enjoy herself. That was quite understandable, and it was her choice.

The downside to this was that Mother gradually withdrew, and little by little she stopped going out except to visit her doctor, the naturopath, and the chiropractor. She did keep in touch with some people over the phone. Overall, she was still pretty happy. During that time twenty years ago, when I was helping my parents, we'd helped them sell their small acreage property, deal with a major council issue that almost prevented the sale, and helped them move up the coast to a blissful life by the water. It was then that we decided to move nearer to them.

We moved there for three reasons. It was a beautiful area with good schools and many services. Our daughter could go to one of those good schools. My husband also said, "You'll be closer to your mother, so you can be there for her." What I didn't realize at the time was that I would be needed there for my father as well, and we became close as a result. My daughter and husband became closer with them too, and later they would help with looking after them. It wasn't a task because my parents were easygoing and nice. We all got along so well together and had fun.

At the time, it was a good thing to do. We found a great home in a beautiful area, and my daughter, my husband, and I met some good people and made friends easily. Life was busy and full of positive things. With our daughter's growing interests in dance, we further enhanced our social lives. Life gradually became even busier as my parents aged and needed more assistance, but I didn't mind. The important thing was that they were looked after, and now they could afford services if needed, such as a cleaner and a gardener. This helped a lot. Later on, we arranged for a nursing service to call at the house. It was mainly for Dad initially, and he preferred it that way. He chose to have qualified professional help come to his home, he enjoyed conversing with the nurses during their visits, and he felt reassured.

My husband worked long hours, and our daughter began home schooling. It was a good choice for her because it complemented the addition of more dance classes and excursions. It was a very special time for us. Our daughter's passion for dancing grew, in particular with modern and ballet. She had a natural talent and a genuine interest. Later she even went on to teach dance classes, and people loved her beautiful nature. We were so proud, and my father would come to her concerts every year. He didn't miss one until it became difficult for him to sit for a long time on a hard chair. I was so grateful that he showed support and went along for many years, and so was my daughter. Some of those concerts were long, but he always wanted to show up. He and my daughter were close. We were close with my mother too, and we proudly showed her the concert DVDs afterward.

My mother also loved to do ballet and tap classes when she was younger. She loved having dance lessons as a child and often spoke fondly of them. Unfortunately, she would then describe how it all abruptly stopped when she was eight, and her mother suddenly died. It was such a young age to lose your mother, and by all accounts she was a good mother. I think Mom received her kind nature from her mother.

As time went on, one day I thought to myself, "This is what I've read about." I recalled an article I had read recently, and it was based on how middle-aged people today, especially those who had children later in life as I did, found themselves in a position where they were getting pulled in different directions. They had to put on a few different hats: mother to a young teenager, assisting two aging parents, running two households, having a husband who worked long hours, and more. There had been a lot to do, from the time it began, when my parents decided to move and downsize. Every week my daughter and I would meet up with my parents, and we viewed many properties before they found one they both loved. Then we helped them organize their move.

Back then Dad was a bit of a hoarder, as most men were who had large properties. I fondly recall him saying, "One day you might need that thing," and he was right about that. The needs of my parents increased as they grew older and more dependent. I liked helping them, and my parents were lovely people; we shared a sense of humor and had fun in the process. Dad was always adamant, especially later on, about how he didn't want to move to a retirement village or an aged care facility. Mother certainly would not have liked all the people. That was all perfectly fine with me. As long as they were happy, it didn't worry me at all, and we managed very well.

However, gradually it hit me one day how well people adapt. When I thought, "Oh, yes, I've read about this. I'm in that age bracket where you have a child or children later, usually because you had a career, and then your parents start needing more and more help." When you combine the two, your life becomes really busy due to looking after everyone. But that was perfectly fine; I loved them all and wanted to make sure they were well looked after.

I adapted my life to suit the situation. I prioritized and became highly organized. It's amazing how much one can manage that way. It was fortunate I didn't have to work at the time because my husband earned a good income.

There was one other thing that I started to think about. At my stage in life and at my age, some mothers would go back to work or start a business, to ensure their financial freedom later in their lives. Considering all my responsibilities, it was impossible to stretch myself that far and still do everything well. I didn't have the time to help everyone, including my parents, and to take my daughter to classes, birthday parties, excursions, and everything else. If I did go back to work or start a business at that time, it was obvious to me I wouldn't be the type of mother I wanted to be, and I wouldn't have the time and patience to assist my parents. It was important to have the time to help them facilitate their lives in a productive way. I knew I could start another business later, just as I had before.

At one point I thought, "Are my parents safe and secure?" Then a lovely aunt of mine who was visiting with us at my parents' house said a curious thing as she was leaving. She turned to me and said quietly, "You must be concerned about their security."

I replied, "It's okay. My mother just had an alarm installed." But her words stayed with me, and as my parents grew older and my father became frailer, it was constantly on my mind.

My parents were financially comfortable, and they had prepared their wills some twenty years before, with their lawyer. They nominated me to be the executor. My parents' assets had grown through good management to be worth over one million dollars. Quite possibly by the time they reached their later years, due to the location of their home, it could have been worth more like $1.5 million. They were secure financially, but their safety did begin to concern me. A representative from the Department of Veterans Affairs suggested a retirement village with care options at one stage, but my father was most adamant: he didn't want to go there, or to any other care or retirement village.

I recall thinking at that time, "I will do my best to look after my parents and help them." Fortunately, thanks to some good financial planning, I also thought, "If they need to dip into their money for their living expenses, their health, their lifestyles, their aged care requirements, or whatever they wanted to do really, well, so be it. It's their money, and they can easily afford it." Even though they wanted to leave an inheritance to their loved ones, it was also their money to look after them in their later years.

It was obvious to me that I could go back to work and start a business later, when my parents weren't with us anymore. I decided to be there for them, for as long as they needed me. But the nagging thought would still crop up occasionally about their security. We certainly had enough services visiting their home, and all the boxes were checked and ticked. With everything their health care people suggested, we looked into it and arranged it. It's only natural I hoped they'd be safe. I recall a few times that I hoped we had covered all the bases and they would be safe and secure in the home they loved.

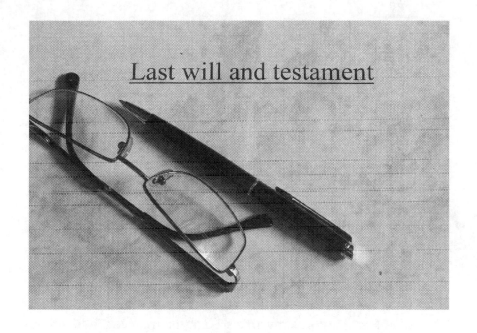

Last will and testament

4

The Dilemma in Relation to Assessment

When Older Parents Seem Upset

To be truthful, looking back, although I was aware of my parents, my husband, our daughter, and I all having a good life, I don't think I fully appreciated just what a lovely time it was in our lives. About six years ago, my parents started to become unsettled. For about fourteen years, they had been leading relatively happy lives since they'd moved and Dad had retired. Now, however, they seemed to be upset. Their contentment with life was disrupted for some reason. There seemed to be something bothering them, an underlying issue, and for some reason they were having difficulty articulating the details.

The issue wasn't about my Dad's Parkinson's; we'd addressed everything he needed to look into for managing his health needs. We had already attended an eight-week comprehensive course specially prepared by the Parkinson's unit at one of the main hospitals. It was a very informative course, and knowledge plus regular appointments with trained specialists is important with this disease. When Dad was asked whether he would like to attend the course, he invited me to attend as his carer. The carers and caregivers were educated as well, as part of the program. As a result, he was indeed informed and prepared, and he had all his specialists and nursing staff in place. They even sent qualified occupational therapists to assess my parents' house and ensure it would be suitable for my father, resulting in them installing some additional handrails and equipment.

The problem also did not appear to be about my mother's health, because her doctor had kindly agreed to do home visits. Mum's doctor made a special exception for her and went to their house, and her doctor and I would e-mail each other if anything needed to be done, such as prescriptions, tests, or medical treatments. I believe now there are services where doctors will do home visits; it's part of an overall plan to assist older people who stay in their homes, if that is what they want to do, and many choose this for reasons that suit them. It was my understanding at the time that it was encouraged (where appropriate of course), in order to help minimize the huge cost associated with senior care.

Thanks to some great medical treatments being offered, the issue wasn't about Dad's recent diagnosis of bowel cancer either. I thought it might have been this initially, because it would of course be upsetting, but he actually handled it well, especially after we took him to the many specialists. When my father was offered a mild treatment that could extend his life for six months to two years, he was happy about that and told me he wanted to proceed. There was another bonus that followed when Dad accepted the offer of treatment from his cancer specialist: he was then offered an additional new treatment as well. Due to the very good results they were seeing with this other new treatment, it was highly likely the outcome would be much more favorable for my father. He had one of the best specialists available, and things were looking positive.

The issue also wasn't about the fact that we were in the process of moving closer to my husband's work. My husband, my daughter, and I had to make the difficult decision. It was becoming almost impossible for my husband to continue commuting due to the increased traffic and the length of time he was driving, plus the much longer hours at work. It was necessary for his safety on the road and the safety of other people. We found a small acreage property near where we used to live, and it was only an hour away from my parents, so that wasn't a large concern. We worked out how everything regarding my parents' care and living arrangements could continue to be easily coordinated; my parents would still be cared for just as well, if not better. Now we had more medical assistance visiting the house. We found out many other people who lived in our area would drive back and forward frequently to the Lake, just like us.

I asked my father whether he'd like to move with us, but he said politely, "No, thanks, Anne. Your mother likes it here by the water." I knew how much my mother loved it there, and Dad had grown to love it just as much. I had already organized all their services, and I followed up on things daily, sometimes spending a couple of hours each day coordinating and checking details, including arranging to have my parents' groceries delivered. I ordered them online each week. They seemed to take great delight in telling me what they wanted each week, and my mother would tell me bluntly if she didn't like anything. A small smile still comes across my face when I think about how she would proudly ring me each week with their grocery order. They also ordered meals from a service called Meals on Wheels. Dad loved them and enjoyed a brief talk with the people who delivered the meals.

There's a key component regarding my parent's happiness and lifestyle. It's something worth bearing in mind, and it relates to how I assisted them. My involvement with my parents was to act as a facilitator, and sometimes like a project manager. I would help them look at their options, but they always made their own choices; I was merely helping to make it happen. When making decisions, often they'd ask, "What do Esme and George do?" Esme and George were my husbands' parents, and they did seem to make good choices. They kindly shared that information with us. My parents enjoyed hearing what they did, and more often than not, they made similar choices about aspects of their lives.

A short while after we'd bought the new property, I noticed my mother had started saying some odd things, and my dad had a little cry as we left his specialist's room one day. I thought it was possibly about the cancer diagnosis, but I wasn't sure. My mother had been saying some odd things for a year or so, which might have been the onset of some form of diminished capacity, or perhaps the early stages of dementia. She was becoming forgetful and had to write herself notes, but it wasn't extreme enough to be overly concerned about it. Dad and I were the ones managing the financial matters, along with their financial advisor, so we weren't too concerned about that.

The comments my mother had started to make more recently were different in that she wasn't just upset about something; she didn't (or couldn't) articulate what it was about. This was in addition to her forgetting important things that grandmothers simply don't forget. Some grandfathers might, but not this proud grandmother. They were both very proud of their family, and they were proud of themselves and their lives. Then one day while waiting in the doctor's waiting room, my mother began speaking in a loud voice about a woman's appearance sitting near us. I distracted her and quickly changed the subject. That was not my mother's usual way; before, she would have been more respectful. I thought at the time that my mother's doctor visited her regularly and would possibly say something if she became concerned. Perhaps I'd look into this as soon as I had Dad's new treatment in place with his doctors and with the nursing service who visited the house (which by this time was twice daily).

Here I were, my family in the throes of moving ourselves. It was just before Christmas, and it was dance concert time as well. I was taking my father to his numerous medical appointments, in order to get him the best health care available with the best specialists. I had to go with them to such appointments, be present, and be a support for them. I saw how one staff member was dismissive of my father because she was busy and didn't seem to appreciate his Parkinson's symptoms. He looked older, and my father's voice was soft due to his Parkinson's; he was slow to answer sometimes. There are two types of Parkinson's, and fortunately for Dad, he had the milder one without the tremors or shaking. It did appear to age him considerably, though, and his movement slowed over time. My point is, when taking an elder to some of those clinics, they are really busy, and an older person can find it a little overwhelming dealing with everything unless he has a helper present with him. It does help for you to attend these appointments with your elder.

The other reason for going with them to medical appointments is that you seem to have to wait a long time in waiting rooms when seeing specialists. Perhaps it felt like that because of the nature of my father's appointments at that time. A cancer diagnosis can be a lengthy process, until one gets all the information. After going for all the tests, then there's the waiting time until you get the results, and then you go back for more appointments. Mind you, on the whole, I also saw a lot more marvelous people working in the medical profession who did their jobs well and looked after elders with great care and respect. A few of the right kind words from them can instantly make someone feel better about a medical condition. The workers really should receive more recognition for all the important work they do.

I remember one medical receptionist who took the time to say to me, "This is how you walk with an older person: just put your arm through his, to be able to support him if needed as you walk." I thanked her kindly when we left, but Dad told me later he didn't like that; he liked to walk on his own two feet without assistance. Dad was "old school," and he'd been a medic in the Korean War. He had been the one who had always looked after the family. It was important to him that he maintained his dignity, his self-respect, and his independence. He also explained to me he didn't like people hanging on his arm because with the stiffening of his joints and movement as a result of the Parkinson's, he found it easier and preferred to find his own balance. For him, having someone holding his arm actually put him off balance. He kindly explained this to me; it was his nature to be a gentle, caring person.

Considering all that was going on at the time, it's fair to say we were a little stretched, but we still managed everything perfectly well. Having patience and paying attention to the details was key. I was good at prioritizing and coordinating many things at once. Having established a reputable public relations consultancy when I was working in Auckland and Sydney instilled the necessary skills to perform many tasks at once and be a good time manager. Plus, I had managed it all successfully for many years, effectively coordinating several different projects at one time, for each of my clients in a calm and thoughtful and professional manner. That ability certainly placed me in good stead to easily coordinate all my parent's activities and arrangements for them, in addition to my own family's needs.

At this particular time, because we were so preoccupied with sorting out the treatment for Dad, I did say to Mum, "I'm sorry if I'm a little distracted with Dad right now, but it's just while we sort out exactly what's happening with his health and work out his options with the doctors." She understood, but she still seemed to be unsettled, and I couldn't quite work out why. When her doctor first started visiting the house to see Mum, she, the doctor, and I decided to get a special notebook that Mum's doctor could make notes in during each visit; Mum could keep it on the table in her room. She liked that plan and felt reassured.

My mother did spend a lot of time in her room, however it was very large, with a water view, a television and telephone, and everything she wanted to have in there. She had most things, including all her craft project supplies, and she was happy with how she'd organized it. More recently, though, Mother kept saying to me, "Look what my Doctor wrote in my book." She appeared a little upset, yet somehow I don't think it was really so much about what the doctor had written in her notes.

I recall explaining at the time, "I know what's in there, Mum. It's okay, because your doctor e-mails me the same details, and if anything needs to be checked or if any tests need to be done, then I know all about it." I'm not sure she quite understood what an e-mail was, but she knew we communicated and was happy about that.

This is the difficult thing. I'm not an expert in this field, and I'm not a doctor. At some point, though, in helping care for elderly parents, the dilemma of whether to approach the subject of having an aged care assessment done may come up. It may only be the little things that add up, but they can grow and become bigger issues for some. It's something to bear in mind, in case it becomes necessary, and it may help head off problems down the track, if a person's capacity begins to diminish to some extent and some form of action needs to be taken. There's a very important and key thing to keep in mind here, when considering whether you should have an assessment done. People seem to hesitate because they don't feel good about doing this to parents whom they love.

However, if you have concerns about an elder parent or both, it may help to prevent financial abuse. If you have a medical assessment that indicates they have lost capacity in some way, and it's dated, then you have proof and can present it if someone takes advantage of them financially. It could make a huge difference if you ever need to step in legally. It is just in case anyone might attempt to manipulate or swindle them out of their money or their assets. The people trying to do this would of course be breaking the law, because it is against the law to have people sign legal documents or to take advantage of them, when they have lost the capacity to manage their financial affairs. At least, that is my understanding and how it was explained to me. Knowing this could be a key component and could be absolutely imperative to helping protect an elder person from financial abuse.

The possible financial abuse that an assessment could play a role in preventing could consist of coercion to sign legal documents or change a will, or even signing for withdrawals for large sums of money. The examples are many, and unfortunately it happens all too often to our seniors. Some months earlier, I met up with someone I knew, and he explained how he was so upset when some people essentially took over his uncle's affairs. He was very close with the uncle, who had recently become terminally ill. It was a sad story, and there were many lies told to the elderly, unwell uncle. My friend described what happened, and he was in tears while explaining how it was all orchestrated as ruthlessly and quickly as a hostile corporate takeover. These people moved into the older gentleman's house, and that man died thinking his nephew had done the wrong thing. He died believing the lies told by the people who had manipulated him and convinced him to sign over his worldly possessions to them before he passed away.

This type of story is not uncommon. These perpetrators want to gain control of the assets, and in turn the money. For some, they want it fast because they're experiencing financial difficulties; others seem to be motivated by greed and having control. They approach the older people and then manipulate or abuse them for their own financial gain. Based on all the stories I've been told, a situation can occur where some people whom an older person may have generously helped out previously ruthlessly take over the elders' affairs and money when they become frailer.

Some of them may think they can do something with the money, but the money may quickly be lost due to the poor schemes in which they invest. They may act alone or in a group of two or three people. It may be done in such a way that it goes undetected. If they come across some opposition to what they're doing, they may embark on a campaign of lies to cover up their real intentions and activities.

It would be fair to say that a huge percentage of the population is made up of good, kind people who would be aghast at this absurd and improper behavior.

Statistics indicate that in addition to the wealth abusers being someone the elders may know, perhaps posing as a financial expert or masquerading as a carer, there's a higher rate reported of the acts being committed by the elders' own children or family members. For many adults the world over, their children are so important to them, and some people may even go as far as to say, "My kids are my purpose, my family, my world." Perhaps for this reason, that is why the abuse is not reported as much as it could be. Consider for a moment how that would make an elderly person feel. To have given your life's work to support and care for your family, and then toward the end the family commits the ultimate betrayal. It would surely have a devastating effect on that elder.

5

The Complications of Stepping In

The Process toward a Hearing

Stepping in to assist the elders in their lives can be a reasonably direct process for some people. Perhaps they may have noticed their mother had shown obvious signs of dementia. They may have received concerned messages from a bank about the elderly parent withdrawing large amounts of money. Then when it becomes obvious for the reason that the parent's safety is at risk, the children know without doubt it is time to step in. At some point, it becomes obvious what needs to be done. This can make the decision easier in some ways, when an adult child who is looking out for elderly parents is advised one of their parents laid on the floor for hours, or a day or two, because he or she had a fall and couldn't get up to call anyone.

But what of the elder parents who exhibit mild, much less obvious behaviors, such as becoming vague, forgetting things, and not seeming to understand their financial situation? These elders can still lead a life at home, but they need to be watched over more than before. How do we assist them in the best way possible? By all accounts, if you don't already have a letter from a medical professional stating they've lost capacity in some way, or you if you don't have an aged care assessment, it may be a very complicated process trying to step in when the elder suddenly becomes at risk of being abused for money or assets.

For some elderly parents, they don't see the need to protect themselves. They've managed perfectly well all their lives; they have been independent, raised a family, and are financially secure—all thanks to how they managed their lives. They could find it an insult to be approached by their adult children to have an assessment done, or to suggest they move into an aged care facility. It can be a difficult time for the adult child who is looking out for aging parents. Deciding what to do and how it should be done becomes complicated and sometimes is a huge ordeal for all involved. One of my older neighbors described in a matter-of-fact way what she and her husband did when they reached their sixties. They retired to a lovely area and liked it there, and when a very smart retirement village was built across the road some years later, they simply moved in there. "It was easy," she said.

Unfortunately, it's not always that simple. For some people, when they suddenly find out one or both of their parents are being subjected to financial abuse, it can be a nightmare to step in, not only for them but for their family as well. Plus, in the case when it's one of their own family members they suspect is abusing the elders, it can be a very complicated situation. Understandably, the tribunals or courts can be reluctant to step in unless you have absolute proof. Then when they get proof, such as a confirmation from the real estate agent that the house is about to be sold, the courts can require a letter from a medical professional or an aged care assessment stating that the elderly person has lost capacity in some way. Sometimes getting that letter is an easy process; it may already have been discussed with the older person's medical team, or it may already be on record.

If not, and if the medical people aren't sure of the situation, it can present a huge problem and make it a very difficult path, trying to navigate to a hearing with a court or tribunal. The adult child helping care for an elder parent or parents may suddenly be thrown into a world of constantly being on the phone, talking with lawyers, doctors, and other medical professionals, trying to get the advice and assistance needed for a hearing in order to step in and stop the wealth abuse. In addition, sometimes because of the details surrounding the abuse of some elders, it can be too difficult to prove in a court or hearing. The elders may or may not want to seek legal action if it's a family member abusing them. However, it's often the only way to stop the wealth abuse, which can often become worse as time passes.

Sometimes the only way is to work with a lawyer who has experience in elder law, and perhaps to also seek advice from a reputable barrister. Then family members may be advised to seek a hearing with the tribunal in that state. In such cases, the only way might be to apply for guardianship of the elder. In certain situations, a lawyer may advise the people seeking help to talk with their parent (if they can) about the application to the tribunal. This prepares the elder, who usually knows by this time he or she is being abused. More important, the elder knows something is being done to step in, and he or she is not being left alone in that situation. But by all accounts, you do need to move quickly, because you need to take into account that people in those situations are elders. They often can't deal with too much stress very well.

If the person seeking assistance is successfully appointed as a legal guardian, he can then legally take steps to stop the elder person being financially abused any further. If it is unsuccessful for whatever reason—perhaps he couldn't produce documented proof, or the perpetrators persuaded or coerced the elder person to lie in order to protect them—there can be many twists and turns. The situation may only worsen, and the trail of wealth abuse can continue unchecked until the elder person's money is depleted. That elder person may or may not understand how and could find himself in a situation where he is fearful of being out on the streets, because that's what he is being told by the person or people abusing him. Then somehow along the way, he may find himself in the predicament where he's actually lost his home as a result.

It can be like an ongoing nightmare for some, especially for the elder people and for those trying to step in. Stepping in sounds easy enough, but it can be very complicated. The other concern while this is occurring is the state of the elders' health. It can be a very stressful time for them, and often they may have been told many lies, making them upset. The perpetrators generally aren't too concerned about doing this to elders. The ones trying to step in are concerned, because they actually care about the elders' welfare and safety.

It can also be a difficult situation for the medical professionals to address. In certain situations, they may be asked to write a letter to a tribunal or for a court hearing, and if they have been lied to by the perpetrators, they may not be sure what is happening and do not know whether to write a letter at all. It is for this reason that they might only want to state it is "a family dispute." Saying it's a family dispute may not be enough to get a hearing for the matter. Instead, the courts usually want to see words relating the capacity of the elder person being diminished in some way, and this will need to be stated in the letter. This is why it could be a good idea to consult with your lawyer on the matter, or one with experience in elder law, and seek the appropriate advice.

You may think it sounds easy, or that surely you can do something. The elders involved may be counting on someone to step in; they may feel intimidated and threatened by the wealth abusers, and so they are reluctant to speak up. If you can successfully step in—and in time to stop the erosion of their assets and their well-being—it's highly likely the elders will be most grateful that you did. In certain cases, not only will the elders have a trusted guardian appointed to protect them in the future, but they will have their lives back, as well as the freedom to live their lives fully without having to be fearful of the perpetrators.

A letter stating the elders have either lost capacity to manage their affairs, or that they could easily be coerced given their background, should be acceptable. However, it is difficult to get these letters sometimes, even though it seems such an easy thing to do. If it is difficult, then there's another possibility. If you can find a medical specialist who works with elders—perhaps one with experience in financial abuse cases—he can be in a more informed position to assist. He has seen this many times before and knows how to read the signs. He would know how to look at the elders' reactions and behaviors and how to hold a conversation with the elders to uncover the truth of the matter.

For some medical people, it could be difficult when they do not know their patients' family, or who is telling the lies, and the care providers could be concerned about possible legal action. But when these elders are having their lives and money hijacked by some unscrupulous dealings, there surely needs to be a better way to deal with this. Some of these older people are not only having their money taken, but their medications may be interrupted or not given correctly. The use of morphine in the hands of the perpetrators can raise some very big questions, and again, it's difficult to prove how it has been administered. In that case, especially when the elders may take medication for a life-threatening illness, a reckless perpetrator may not even give them the medications they need. Sometimes it's difficult to know who the abusers are until it's too late.

From the elders' point of view, they need to feel safe and confident that they are secure. With my own father, I had met with his doctor numerous times before, when I took Dad to his appointments. But the doctors are very busy, and in some of the large clinics they must see hundreds of patients each week. I do fondly recall, when taking Dad to his doctor's appointments for checkups, we had an arrangement with his doctor where I would step out of the room when it came time for his doctor to do a physical examination. Dad was a proud man, and the doctor and I respected that. I enjoyed looking out for my father. He had a great sense of humor, and he was one of those older people around whom one felt good. It was a bit like in the movie *The Holiday*, where the young woman befriends a neighboring older gent, and they have a fun time. They go out for a meal, share a joke, and enjoy each other's company, just as so many civilized people do.

Looking back, as my father became frailer, I knew he still had the capacity to make his own decisions, but because he was so frail, he could have been coerced by some overpowering person. One of the symptoms of Parkinson's is that elders can become fearful or wary, and his eyesight was failing in his later years. It's difficult to know what to do sometimes. If I had asked earlier for him to be assessed, he might have been insulted. I remember once when taking him to the bank, I had the real estate contract with me for the sale of our home. He spoke out of character and said to me, "What are they for?" in a slightly accusing tone. When I explained they were for my house, he relaxed. Sometimes you don't want to upset elders unnecessarily, but in some cases, steps might need to be taken in order to protect them.

If at some stage you find you need to have an elder assessed, there's no need to feel guilty about it if you do. Remember, you may actually be protecting them. When I initially heard of this suggestion and thought of my own parent's security, my immediate reaction about my father was to think, "But he does have capacity, and I wouldn't want a letter like that being used by the wrong person to put him in care." I didn't understand fully at that time how having an assessment can work in order to maintain elders' level of care and safety. I realize now that it can be very important to have so that you can prevent them from being abused financially and emotionally. It could quite possibly save you and the elders you're helping a lot of heartache at some later stage.

Perhaps there should be more education about this area of wealth abuse for the medical profession, so that they fully realize the extent and the complications in preventing wealth abuse. For people generally, it would greatly assist with the issues of wealth abuse if something could be done much earlier. It doesn't seem right to me that our elder seniors are sometimes like sitting ducks, and unscrupulous people can come along and coerce or manipulate them the way they do. I'm not an expert, but surely there must be something we can do.

How on earth, in our modern society, are we allowing this to happen? Probably because the majority of people aren't aware of the extent to which it occurs. As socially conscious people, perhaps we need to start asking some serious questions—and as quickly as possible. What is the problem here? How can it be changed? We also need to look for answers, before too many more elder people are abused. Am I the only one seeing this? I don't think so. There seems to be a gaping hole, or rather a gray area, in the structure of our legal systems, making it difficult to protect elders. Is there a way we can effectively create a safety net to ensure they're kept safe? Should there be more education in the mix or on the to-do list? Should the government be looking at a budget allocation to look at the problem and devise a way to install some safeguards for our senior citizens? Should a think tank be created?

This next suggestion seemed an obvious idea to me, although I'm not an expert in this area. Should we consider the possibility of having a central register or something similar set up, where our senior people register their wills? A register of some kind could be effectively checked by lawyers or authorized people in the legal profession to see whether there are already legal documents in place. This may help to prevent the perpetrators telling lies to another lawyer, who may be an innocent party and doesn't know the elderly person. Could this essentially close the gap or address this gray area to some extent? Is it a starting point in the campaign against elder wealth abuse?

Something like this could go a long way to preventing the many situations that occur where the perpetrator effectively manipulates an elderly person into changing the will and leaving everything to the con man. Some elders may not even want to do this, but they're made to feel they have to by the perpetrators, and sometimes they are passively and aggressively abused to sign legal documents. Another example is where they may be abused to sign a power of attorney. As you can well imagine, a power of attorney in the wrong hands can be a license to steal.

6

Being a Voice for the Elders

Our Seniors Should Be Valued

If someone was to voice what elders really thought about wealth abuse, one might hear a few interesting, choice words on the issue. Their comments might range from, "We have paid our taxes all our lives and invested in our families, our countries, and even the world. Considering we hold the much larger portion of the wealth in most developed countries, why isn't something being done about it?" They might also ask, "Why aren't our governments immediately doing something effective to prevent this from happening?" Chances are some of them will be really nice about it and say, "And you think you can trust some people." As the woman I watched being interviewed made the last comment, I could see the deep hurt in her eyes.

Another thing some might say is "I've not recovered from the shock of some of my adult children taking advantage of me in my old age, treating me with such disrespect when I deserve to be respected—and after all I've done for them!" Another might say, "I could perhaps disinherit them because of what they've done. It was as though my opinion didn't matter, and they didn't care what I wanted to do. They've hurt not only me but other members of the family, and they've turned a good situation into a bad one."

Elders might tell you how fired up they are about it. They might raise their fists up in the air at the injustice of it all, just as they might have done many years ago, when they were younger. They might explain how no one seemed to listen or care that financial abuse was happening to them. They might try to hold back the tears that indicate just how upset they actually are about it all. Also, they might tell you how it made them feel worthless, or they might show their absolute disgust, which will be written all over their faces.

You could hear them describe how they were waiting for the person they trusted to step in and arrange a hearing, so they could get the abusers out of their lives and out of their house. Then they might explain, "But days, weeks, and eventually two months went by, and it became obvious they were having difficulties being able to get a hearing even though I told them to proceed. I've been waiting and hoping they'd be successful, and I wanted them desperately to step in and do something that would help me."

Other elders might explain how their loved ones didn't really know what was happening until it was done, and then it became complicated because legal documents were already signed, and money was going missing from the bank account at an alarming rate. They might say, "The people doing it didn't care—they went through all my personal documents as though they had a right to do so, but they didn't!" Then they might add, "It was abuse, clear and simple, but it was done in such a cunning way that people didn't seem to notice."

Another elder may tell you, "Before I knew it, they took over my affairs. They had a real estate agent in to get a valuation on the property, and they were constantly at me every day to sell the house, and to change my will and leave more to them. Sometimes they would even order me to do things, and they'd say things like,

'If you love me, you will give it to me because I deserve it now. I'm looking after you.'" Then the elder might explain how she didn't ask for them to look after her in the first place, or move into her house. When she told them to get out, they refused to leave.

One elder might say, "If my doctor wouldn't give the person I trusted most in the world the letter he needed to get a hearing, then why didn't the doctor write a referral for a geriatrician to come see me? Someone I know did just this and got a hearing."

Another might tell you, "There were so many lies told to the police when they were called the house. They were told they were getting me to sign legal documents, but I couldn't speak because I was so upset and unwell. The cops just left."

There will be some elders with a story about a successful outcome, where the people they trusted realized it in time and stopped the sale of their house. Another good outcome could be the court ruled the money be paid back to the elder person. How elders tell their stories depends on the circumstances in which they were being financially abused.

Perhaps we need to think about collectively helping in order to be that voice for our elder senior citizens. We should be that voice so that in the future, the result will be a better place where perhaps even we and our children will not have to endure the ultimate betrayal. There's a heavy sadness that can set in after something like this has happened. I think it may be because of the unfairness of it all, as well as the feeling of being powerless to do anything about it. It's sometimes difficult to prove, and it can be humiliating and degrading. The way I see it, there's a real huge problem stacking up here. It's a problem elder people shouldn't have to go through, and one they will most likely be unable to change by themselves. They need some help.

I can't help but think there's a need for more education on elder financial abuse, and there should be a clear plan on how to effectively handle a situation like this. Prevention would be ideal, so how should it be done to effectively address this issue? We should be listening more when people speak of this, because someone doesn't just start making accusations like these without a good reason. There is no way they would have spent hours, days, weeks, and perhaps months on this unless there was definitely something going on—something that's against the law!

By the time people become older, they have gained a lot of wisdom and maturity, and usually a great sense of humor. If you listen to what elders have to say, you might learn something and enjoy their company. During the last couple of years before my father passed, we became even closer, and I immensely enjoyed his company. Elders may slow up a little as they age, but their input and contributions to the world should be valued; they should be appreciated and respected. And they have a right to feel safe and secure at this later stage.

My Father's Funeral

I vividly recall the day of my father's funeral. It was not just any funeral, where one attends to pay one's respects. It was the funeral of a very special man who was respected for being a good, generous person, and we loved him dearly. We often heard him say, "She'll be right" - an Australian slang phrase for it'll be okay, and it always was. On this day, I didn't feel like it was right, but the overriding important thing for me that morning of his funeral was to ignore that feeling, and to stand up there and present some beautiful words about my father at the service. He deserved that, and his friends and family present deserved to hear it. Sometimes in his later years, he wasn't always shown the respect he deserved by some as he neared the end of his life; possibly it was due to the difficulties of having Parkinson's. However, I thought he did manage this with dignity, and I was proud of the way he did that.

Looking back, I was so appreciative that some good souls, who knew how difficult it was going to be for us that day, arrived at our house that morning. One close friend, who was recovering from a serious illness herself and was struggling to regain her health, took the day off work and came with us in the car to the funeral. My cousin, her husband, and their daughter arrived at our house and followed us in their car. Two close friends from Sydney also took time off work and drove up the freeway, a two-hour drive one-way, to be there out of respect for my father and to support us. They remembered how, many years ago, my father would drive us around and drop us at the places we wanted to go, before we were old enough to get our driver's licenses. He was always kind, he trusted us and helped us, and we trusted him implicitly.

When it was time to get in the car that morning and drive to Dad's funeral, I noticed we were all quietly and politely going through the motions. I knew how people felt when someone they were really close to passed on. Somehow people manage to keep moving, attend the funeral, and speak at it. I had driven that way to my parents' house many times before, but on this day it seemed to take such a long time. There I was, in the passenger seat of the car this time; my husband was driving, and our daughter and our friend were in the backseat. We drove to the funeral that morning, sitting in silence and still stunned with the knowledge of what had occurred. My father had had a lot to deal with toward the end of his life. He experienced a lot of pain, and cancer toward the end is not a pleasant experience. It felt surreal, like watching a sad movie, only this time we were in it.

Even now, years later, when I think of what happened, my heart feels heavy, my throat chokes up, and tears come to my eyes.

My father and I were always close but became even closer as he aged. He trusted me to do the right thing by him and help him whenever he asked. When we'd say good-bye, he'd hold my hand for a moment; that was his way of saying, "I trust you." It was because I had helped him over the years to create a very comfortable lifestyle for my father and mother, and he knew he could trust me without a doubt. They had become reasonably well off financially and owned a beautiful home. I had played a role in assisting them to do that, and they knew it and appreciated it. It was all coordinated on the basis of mutual respect. Goodness knows my father and mother had certainly helped me when I was younger. Isn't that what being family in the true sense of the word is all about?

It was obvious to most people how my parents loved the home and location they moved to before the increasing health issues, including their lifestyles, the water views, and the safe village atmosphere that contributed to how happy they were. Apparently, as my father intimated to me, he didn't always receive respect from everyone in his later years. My father's nursing staff was full of wonderful people and I recall sometimes being there and noticing how they brightened up his day when they arrived. It's important to an elderly person that he's treated with the respect and dignity he deserves.

Now here we were at my father's funeral. This was the same crematorium he had been to many times before, to say good-bye to his old friends who had passed previously. Many of them were war veterans—returned men and women, they called them. They had been a great support to each other over the years. My father's medical cancer specialist had said with the treatment they'd offered him, he'd have another six months to two years; his outcome could have been quite good, and at least he would have had more time. But that wasn't to be. His treatment could have been even better and more effective than that, because his specialist had offered him the additional new treatment—one they'd seen good results with so far.

The day before I managed to prepare some words to speak at the service, and I wanted to say some truthful words of respect for my father. As we entered the funeral, I remember being so very grateful for our friend, who walked closely behind us holding firmly onto our daughter. This was also my daughter's first funeral. What a way to experience the first funeral you attend; she was quite gentle then and only fifteen years old. Whenever I visited my parents, my daughter was usually with me. She loved Dad as much as I did. How awful would that have been for her, to know to some extent what had happened surrounding my father's last months, and to feel powerless to do anything, it must have been so upsetting for her.

Some years later, when my husband's mother passed, I had to reassure our daughter that attending her lovely grandmother's funeral would be okay. I said because my mother-in-law simply passed away one evening peacefully and not in any pain. Her grandmother's funeral would also have people who loved and respected her there, and we would all say good-bye to her in a dignified manner and be supportive of each other. I wanted to prepare some words to say at her funeral too, just as I did for my own father, because they were both good people, among the best one could ever meet. And so was my husband's father, who had passed some years earlier. My husband's mother was an important person to many; she was like the matriarch of the family. Everyone loved and adored her. I've often thought with my husband's father passing some years before, thank goodness she didn't have to experience the ultimate betrayal.

I clearly remember how, on the day of Dad's funeral, my husband stood tall in his dark suit beside me. It was hard for him too, because he had become good friends with my father over the years. He would often take Dad out on Saturdays for a day out, or take him to the bank or to get some groceries. It was hard for him on this day, but he stood there like a rock beside my daughter, and I was grateful for that.

After walking into the funeral, we were stopped by an imposing gentleman just inside the door, and he said to me, "I believe you want to say something during the service?"

I replied, "Yes, as long as I'm not too upset to do so."

His words were very reassuring; it was something about the way he said it. "I'm sure you'll find the strength."

When the time came to speak, I did. When it was time to stand up there and speak, I pulled out the paper I'd written the words on, along with a beautiful verse they gave us at the hospital. The strength and the words flowed through me so strongly without pausing, and they were powerful. It was out of respect for my father that I stood up there and spoke of the things that were important to hear about him, of the decent person he was and how this world needed more good role models like him.

I recall afterward being so grateful that I chose to say something and prepare words in honor of the man who gave so much during his life. Someone I respect and know well made an interesting observation, and she commented some months after the funeral, "There was only one person during that service who spoke about the good person your father was, the decent man."

My husband also said to me some weeks afterward, "Did you notice, Anne, how after the funeral, as we moved outside, everyone gathered around you?" I did recall that, and it was so lovely. I think they appreciated the words about my father, because they loved him too.

All Dad's friends from his club were there, mostly ex-servicemen, to offer their respects and condolences. Some family members traveled a long way to be there, and I hadn't seen a few in many years. That was a sign of how respected Dad was. I recall how my husband, who knew Dad's war veteran friends well, rang and told them when Dad had passed, to make sure they were involved in the funeral arrangements. He made sure Dad was represented properly. Good on him for doing that; he always knows the right thing to do. Overall it was a lovely funeral, and it was held in a beautiful place. That was the important thing that day.

As we left the wake later, we walked out to the club area, where Dad's friends were gathered, and we spent some time with them. These men and women were good people, mostly war veterans and members of his club. They were worldly people, like my father. There were not as many of Dad's friends left now, sitting at their club at the "Table of Knowledge." It was a good acknowledgment of the type of people who sat there.

7

An Important Overview

Where Does the Family Wealth Go?

Elder financial abuse, in whatever form, is against the law, and the law is appropriately named undue influence. No wonder, then, that perpetrators go to such lengths to cover it up and conceal what they've done. They think they'll get away with it, but there's always someone watching, and the evidence often becomes obvious afterward. Many people don't like what these people do to elders, and neither do the elders. The aware people of the world are incredulous at what is done.

I knew there were some pretty bad people in the world, but I never thought this issue was so widespread. It's hard to live with it, taking all this information into account, but eventually we can find a way to help create a better life for ourselves, and we can create a better life for our elders. We have an opportunity here to do something about it. For those of you who've already suffered from the indignity of elder wealth abuse, I encourage you to try to find some inner strength and go on, even though it does stay with you.

I remember looking elder abuse up on Google, and I found out this low act was actually against the law while reading some of the descriptions. The website www.legal-dictionary.com shows clear descriptions that can be found in *West's Encyclopedia of American Law*. It states, "Undue Influence—A judicially created defense to transactions that have been imposed upon weak and vulnerable persons," and "Virtually any act of persuasion that overcomes the free will and judgment of another, including exhortations, importunings, insinuations, flattery, trickery, and deception." These were parts of their descriptions, and it certainly is worth looking up the actual cases they cite. I often wish I had been more informed about this earlier for many reasons, but the main one was that I could have begun this work sooner.

If you google the word "importuning," you may find descriptions such as "harass (someone) persistently for or to do something," or "demand with urgency or persistence." Based on the accounts of the stories I have heard so far, these two descriptions, along with the other words already mentioned in the previous paragraph are accurate descriptions of what occurs. It is carried out behind closed doors or out of sight, or away from of those who genuinely care for elders and might hear the abuse.

There's another description shown from *West's Encyclopedia of American Law:* "Undue Influence—the amount of pressure which one uses to force someone to execute a Will leaving assets in a particular way, to make a direct gift while alive, or to sign a contract." There are many descriptions, and they are relevant in most countries. When looking into this later on, I also found all these people and organizations. They are advocates of the elderly, and they also think this is a disgraceful thing to do to elder people. They talk about it frankly and in no uncertain terms. Good on them for doing so; maybe it's time we join them so that more can be done about this.

I know at one point I embarked on the concept of creating an organization that could have the effect of a movement of some sort that could campaign to do something about it. At one point

I thought, "This is hard. Do I really want to do this, and can I manage it?" Then the next day I thought, "Yes, I can, and I'm going to. If I can help some other elder people avoid having to go through it, then by all means, I am going to do this!" It was then I recalled the saying "Knowledge is power." Perhaps it's high time a lot more people became knowledgeable about this issue, which more often than not occurs without people speaking out. It's mainly due to the fact the elders are too frail or feel too vulnerable to speak up. We need some key people to stand up and be their voice. Many people are certainly putting their hands up to help.

When I tell people today what happens, and they are not too familiar with elder wealth abuse, their response is often "Oh, surely you must be able to do something." I recall the reaction of one of my parents' helpers when we talked about this issue. She adored my parents, and she mentioned how her friend has also seen many such cases of elder financial abuse. He actually worked in this field of elder care in the UK, and he said it has to be a family member who steps in. I'm not sure about that, but I do know she was so upset that this happens. She loves working with elder people and did a good job keeping my parents' house in order for them. I could tell she genuinely cared for the elders.

Writing this book has been a very hard thing to do. One has to live it in order to be able to absorb all the information and then express what happens. Yes, it's illegal, and when people do this to an elder person, it is against the law. This is why they will go to such lengths to cover it up. I imagine to this day that there are many who think they've managed to get away with it. But there are people out there who don't like what they've done—not at all. The smart people out there are most likely watching the perpetrators, still incredulous and disgusted at the knowledge of what they did. They will know they've told a lot of lies and about what they've done. They possibly hold the same view as I do, and that is "There may be some bad apples in the world, but this is such an injustice!"

My parents had asked for their wills to be drawn up by their long-term lawyer some twenty years ago, when they'd retired, and they regularly checked in with that lawyer to ensure it was still current. They gave the lawyer very specific instructions when the wills were drawn up, and they wanted me to be the executor. They did this when their health, both mentally and physically, was sound and as they were planning for the later stage of their lives. A friend who is a counselor mentioned he always recommends to his clients to choose their most trusted child or person, making him or her the executor and giving power of attorney. That is exactly what my parents did, and it's the choice many other seniors make.

However, what appears to be happening is that perpetrators approach the elders in their later years and coerce or manipulate them into changing the wills. Many elders have lost some capacity by then, and they find it difficult to deal with the antics and constant harassment. Many eventually give in and go along with it because they don't want any more angst. It doesn't mean they approve—they definitely do not! But quite possibly this is where all the family wealth goes. Think about it for a moment, if you will. I know I wondered some years ago. Both my parents came from reasonably wealthy families. They were big property owners, and there was definitely considerable money and assets in the family. So where did it all go? My parents certainly didn't have it. They had to start with nothing and make their own wealth.

My mother's family in particular had considerable property in the Upper Hunter Valley in NSW Australia; it was grazing land, now world renowned for beautiful horse studs and extensive vineyards and wineries. They also had property in Sydney and would play tennis and socialize there regularly. The wealth was considerable not too many generations ago. It is natural to stop and wonder where all the wealth went.

I'm presuming here, because it appears to be difficult to trace. But is this what happens? The scenario could have been that at some late stage, certain family members carried out a ruthless takeover of elders' affairs. Then perhaps shortly afterward, the elders would be so upset and unable to speak about it, and they would give up and pass away, feeling completely degraded, humiliated, and upset by what had happened. It could have been too much to deal with, or they simply couldn't stand up to the bully.

Sometimes the family wealth over generations is not in fact lost because of mismanagement or being misplaced; it is in fact taken by means of undue influence—meaning it's taken illegally. Some of these seniors are left feeling absolutely devastated if they become aware they've been swindled. In the case of the elders with limitations, they may be left wondering where their money went. They may say something like "I don't know what happened. I thought I had more money. I must have been mistaken."

Elder Seniors with Limitations

There are elders who perhaps could be described as noninstitutionalized adults who may need help with their living arrangements or personal care. Perhaps they have basic or complex activity limitations. According to the statistics, there are many millions of adults living in our communities with at least one basic action difficulty or complex activity limitation.

Sadly, people with disabilities get abused. Sometimes those disabilities are not too obvious, but these elders may lack the skills to be aware of managing their finances and could easily be taken advantage of. They can be especially vulnerable to financial abuse, and they can easily be manipulated or be subjected to passive-aggressive verbal abuse. They may not know how to deal with it or even report it.

As you can well imagine, they can also easily be coerced or verbally manipulated to change their wills, being persuaded to pay for expensive items, to lend money without it being repaid, to sign over ownership of a home, or to give someone power of attorney. A legal document such as a power of attorney can be a very useful tool and an effective way for an elder to ask someone to help with his or her financial affairs. That is, if that someone is trusted and truly does help. In the hands of someone capable of financial abuse, it could be a license to steal money.

There is another scenario to consider. If a person with limitations, especially concerning financial matters, survives a marriage where the partner may have managed all the financial affairs, the elder can then become vulnerable to being abused for wealth. To understand the full picture about these types of situations is to also realize they can be complicated.

Keep Track of the Paper Trail

During the course of the time I actively helped my parents build their wealth and their lifestyles, they loved it all and were content. That was my gift to them. The thought that someone could come along and use some form of undue influence probably didn't even occur to them. We had a paper trail, and it just seemed to work out that way, probably because that was always how I'd managed my own life, as did my father. A paper trail was simply good record keeping. Looking back, that was probably reassuring for my parents. Or in my parents' case, perhaps it was more reassuring for my father because he was the one who managed their financial affairs during the course of their lives together, and later with my assistance.

There's Nothing Wrong with Having Wealth

It occurred to me at some point that if seniors didn't have the wealth they did, perhaps they could avoid experiencing wealth abuse. But that's an absurd notion. There is nothing wrong with having money, and money can be a good thing. In fact, it's necessary to live in the world as we do. It can help people afford a very enjoyable life, take care of them and their family, and look after them in comfort during their later years. It is to be enjoyed, not to be worried about, because someone might try to take it. We need to work out how to prevent wealth abuse.

I was the eldest child, and from the time I turned eighteen, I often assisted my mother with many things, including embarking on some big cleanup projects around the house or on the property. I did anything to help them. Even when I was younger as a teenager, I recall getting a bad feeling about this one couple. They befriended my parents, moved into a small cottage on our property, and lived there for a while. They appeared nice enough, but trouble sure seemed to follow these people.

After a couple of months, they left in a hurry in the middle of the night, owing money. I remember Dad saying, "I think they're going to do a runner," the day before they left, and that is exactly what they did. Oddly enough, they even returned some years later to try it again, but by then I was older, and they could see I saw right through their plan. Plus, I was living in that cottage by then. I had renovated it, and Dad had kindly helped me whenever I needed a hand. The couple left that day, and they didn't ever make contact again. However, my mother had welcomed them on that return visit, and she appeared happy to see them and seemed unaware of what they'd done on their previous stay. But my father knew, and he was aware of the type of people they were.

We didn't have a lot of money back then, however my parents did own their small acreage property, and they could possibly have been manipulated over time. Fortunately, that didn't happen; I don't think my father would have allowed that. I recall what it was like then to not have enough money to do the things I really wanted to do in life. It is far more fulfilling to have enough money to lead a life that brings you enjoyment, whether that includes travel, buying the type of car you want, or choosing how you want to live your lifestyle. It is less stressful, and you feel more comfortable when you don't have to worry about not having enough. Back then, while I was in my teenage years, I clearly remember witnessing my mother becoming withdrawn, and this was quite possibly because they didn't have a lot of spare money for lifestyle things that a lot of people took for granted. They had enough for food and some clothing, but not much more.

I often recall the small rural property that my parents owned those many years ago, the one on which I grew up. It would sometimes become very messy, as would the house, or it would become run down. I clearly remember the huge effort I put into tidying things up; renovating the bathroom, lounge, and kitchen; and cleaning up outside around the house. Dad would help when he wasn't working; he always helped whenever he could. He did the shopping, paid the bills, and kept everything afloat. On some level, my mother didn't feel confident or motivated to do this property improvement work, so sometimes she would ask me, and sometimes I would simply decide to do things to make it better for her. Often I would buy her flowers to cheer her up.

There are numerous stories like this one. As a close friend once said to me, "You had to be the grown-up in your family." Yes, I suppose that was true to some extent. I was the eldest, I had good instincts, and I was mature and responsible. I do remember clearly that when I was a child, my father was always working, often two or even three jobs to support us. He was a good person, and he always looked out for people. He was one of the most decent people I've met, and he was a good worker. Always on the go, he worked tirelessly, and he certainly didn't lack any motivation back then.

When Dad was young, his father died when he was about twelve. Dad became the man of the family because he was the eldest of eight children. But it wasn't just because he was the eldest; it was in his nature to offer assistance to anyone who needed a hand. I recall his sister, the youngest and only girl, describing how he built her a swing. He was always kind and generous. Even in his later years, I recall how he helped a friend of mine who lived on a property and was becoming upset. She was isolated and without power for days, after a major storm followed by a widespread electricity blackout. She didn't even have the means to make a cup of tea. All the gas bottles had sold out everywhere, and people were getting desperate because the whole area experienced a major power failure with no sign of it being rectified soon. Dad quietly went to his garage and gave me his spare gas bottle to give to her. He didn't know her, but that was the type of man he was.

8 The Makings of the Guide

The Result of Everyone's Stories

It was a couple of years after my father passed, before I could even start to feel happy and productive again. I've heard many people explain that they felt this way, and in fact it's quite common, especially when you were close. You may feel fine and function perfectly well, but something inside you is flat, and you lack motivation. I've realized since talking with other people that it's perfectly normal to feel this way, but you do get your life back on track, and the enthusiasm gradually returns.

It was about this time that I found myself sitting in my office preparing to start speaking about elder financial abuse, and to lobby to see whether we could effectively improve things. I was speaking with a friend, who was also concerned with matters of the world and looking out for people generally. We talked about the obvious blatant abuse and my concerns with how widespread it appears to be. She said to me, "I think you should write a guide."

I recall thinking at the time, "Good idea, but how on earth would I do that?" Yet here I am today, actually doing it three and half years later. I'm setting up an enterprise and an organization modeled to do just that, and a lot more! Now I'm driven by the fact that I've obtained all this information over the last couple of years, and it has led me to believe that when wealth abuse occurs, it hits the victims hard.

If it happens to your own parents or grandparents, it hits you even harder, especially when everything you do to step in is headed off by the perpetrators. In some cases, it appears the offenders might have someone helping them who has knowledge of how the legal system works. It's as though the people who do this are one step ahead. This is why it stays with you. You hear all the details of how elders have been abused, and how the offenders have made the elders cry and have verbally abused them into signing documents. You don't easily forget the persistent, ongoing abuse and the overwhelming verbal abuse that is done to a huge number of elders. The memory of it stays with you. And with all the people who describe their stories, it undoubtedly stays with you.

I seemed to function well afterward, after all the time spent investigating the details and hearing all the stories people told me, but everything felt so hard to do. This was unknown territory for me, and naturally it was very upsetting. Fortunately I'm a strong person with a good support network, including my family and a group of friends, and they helped a lot. They didn't enjoy seeing me upset by all of this, but they understood the underlying importance of this work and supported what I set out to do. The countless and decent professional people I've met along way who offered words of encouragement and assistance were also appreciated and compelled me to keep going.

To be honest, I'm not sure how a more gentle person would cope with all this information, all these stories of elder abuse, or even when elder abuse happened to her personally. I remember clearly what it felt like during and after listening to all the details and reading everything. It wasn't pleasant, and it did have the affect of dragging me down. Now the difference is I'm conscious of making the choice to turn that knowledge into something that makes a difference. Creating more awareness will be the key component to actually succeeding.

By all accounts, those experiencing wealth abuse for the first time can feel as though they are suddenly being catapulted into a life that is going horribly wrong. In some cases, everything they do to help the elders doesn't seem to work or can take so long. They can find they are up against some hardball players who know exactly what they're doing because they've done it before, or because they've been well briefed by other people who have done it before. It does gradually become evident when the onslaught of abusive and defamatory behavior is carried out against people who are innocently caring for the elders. The offenders do this to weaken them so that they can have access to the elders concerned. It can be an enormous thing on many levels to deal with sometimes.

I recall one lawyer describing when he heard of the enormity of how this was affecting his elderly clients, and how the wealth abuse tactics became overbearing. He said, "Oh, this is way out of my league!" He referred those clients to another lawyer. That can be a horrible time in someone's life. But it must be a lot worse for the elder who is subjected to financial abuse in whatever form— and even more so if the elder involved is unwell or frail. The elders affected could have even looked after the abuser during their lives, because it could be one or more of their own children, trying any tactic they think will work to access the money. Sometimes the tactics escalate as the elders reach their last few months or the last year of their lives. Sadly, the elders usually know exactly what the offenders are doing. They are abusing them to get the money, and if the elders do happen to know them, then quite possibly any respect that may have been shown previously is suddenly gone.

I would imagine most of the elders affected could be similar to my father: someone who has seen difficult times, and so they hope they can trust people later in their lives, especially their own families. You normally won't see elders cry, but when wealth abuse occurs, they do cry, even if on the inside so you don't see the tears. I recall one of the times I heard my father cry, when my mother was rushed to the hospital in an ambulance to the intensive care unit. It wasn't pleasant hearing that. My mother had refused help; she was very ill and wouldn't agree to Dad calling a doctor. She became gradually worse and was barely conscious by the evening. It was then that he decided to call for an ambulance.

There was big scene outside their house that evening; neighbors and passersby had gathered and watched. The paramedics had to call the state emergency service, who had to get a crane there and winch my mother out of the second floor in a stretcher. That was after they'd taken down the railings to eventually get her down to the ambulance. It was due to my mother's size, and because she was semiconscious, they couldn't walk down the steps with her. Dad installed a high-end chair lift for them after that, one that was specially made and would carry the appropriate weight without a problem. No wonder he had a quick cry. It was an ordeal for him, that's for sure, and I can't begin to imagine how it must have been for my mother. I knew everything because we were speaking on the phone as the ambulance was leaving, and we then arranged for my husband to call in to check whether my father was okay. I planned to go the hospital.

The brief cry he had on the phone that evening was just for a moment; it was a release, a reaction to the stress. My mother had been described as agoraphobic, and she had a fear of going to the hospital and going outside. Little did we know at the time there would be other similar situations that would follow, but fortunately they did not involve being winched out of her house by a crane. Luckily for my mother, considering all the problems, Dad was a very patient man. After this same health problem occurred two more times, we found a medical specialist while she was still in the hospital, and he told her straight, "Either you go and be submitted to a rehabilitation unit for two months, or you die." She agreed. If he hadn't done that, she quite likely would not have survived much longer.

The unfortunate thing for my mother was that following the treatments in hospital numerous times and possibly the high level of antibiotics that were needed, it left her without the desire or ability to read. I recall her saying to me, "Since the times in hospital, I'm not sure if was all the antibiotics, but I just don't want to or can't read books, or anything." That was a shame because she used to love reading books, and half her wardrobe was full of books. We would be so excited to get the latest edition of our favorite author's books, and we'd share them and have conversations about the stories. It's things like this that can occur later in an older person's life that can make them more vulnerable, because they can lose capacity in some way during the later stages.

How Does It Make You Feel?

When people find out about elder financial abuse, especially what was done to the elders in the process, the hurt they felt is difficult to describe. That is what I've been told many times over, and I can certainly understand how that would be so. Dad and I were close, and I eventually helped him with most things later in his life. He trusted me, and with good reason. For those people who've witnessed what this form of abuse does to an elder, it can be devastating.

Hearing of this is upsetting enough. It's worse when people think about how it unfolded right in front of them, and whatever they tried to do to help didn't work! It can be a very harsh experience.

Then when they find that some people doubt what they're saying, it can make it even harder. Friends may know that they wouldn't lie, but perhaps they wonder whether they might be somehow getting it wrong. It all sounds so horrendous and cruel. Some people are disgusted when they hear of elder abuse. But the lawyers know about it all too well, and they have seen this happen many times before.

After I learned of this, it completely changed the course of my life. I was planning to go to back to college and obtain a health sciences degree. In fact, I did enroll to do just that, but I couldn't focus. Every time I tried, I kept thinking of what happens to these elders, and then I asked myself, "How could people have been more effective at stepping in?" I reached the point where I came to the realization that I had all these skills that could greatly assist others to prevent elder wealth abuse. I have studied, have qualifications, and I have run my own public relations practice. I was the managing director, ran the company for several years, and was good at this line of work. My prominent and reputable clients had retained my services for many years because they trusted me and liked my work. I had all these other skills and qualifications that could also contribute to making a difference and helping people with this area of abuse.

We told one of our good friends about my plan. He said to my husband and me, "It's one of the worst kinds of abuse, Anne."

The question quietly came to me one day. "Why don't I use my professional skills that I've acquired over the years and shift my focus? I should work in the area of wealth abuse awareness and prevention for our senior citizens." It occurred to me that they needed someone to be a voice, to be an advocate for the elderly, to expose the abuse and bring it out into the open. I sought to inform people and create more awareness. Even with all the people who have since confided in me about their stories relating to elder wealth abuse, I still find it hard to fully comprehend how prevalent it is. It's an absolute disgrace that it occurs to the extent it does in our society. Today I still have considerable difficulty with the facts, with the knowledge that this occurs.

In this modern world we live in, the number of incidences is very high and is increasing. At the time of writing this book, elder abuse helplines in Australia were reporting the number of calls had doubled, cases dealing with elderly abuse had increased by 30 percent in the past 12 months (in one state), tripled in another. Some advisors suggested the occurrence rate had doubled to 1 in 10, where the earlier research indicated one in twenty elders are financially abused.

Monash University research commissioned by legal and financial services organization, State Trustees, to shed some light on this 'silent crime', found that up to 5% of Australians over 65 have experienced financial abuse. The research also found that older women over the age of 80 are most at risk and their own children are the most common perpetrators. The more recent results of the Investor Protection Trust [IPT] Elder Fraud and Financial Exploitation Survey indicated that nearly 1 in 5 U.S. seniors are hit by financial swindles.

The number of reports in the media has increased, Inquiries have been conducted and new Inquiries announced, yet still the rate appears to be increasing. Elder Abuse Help Lines are reporting it's increasing. According to an interview broadcasted by the Australian Broadcasting Corporation [ABC], "Lawyers are calling for new, specific laws to deal with the 'hidden' elder abuse, which the Age Discrimination Commissioner says is a 'huge problem' that is getting worse (19/11/2015)". So there it is: The research is there, the reports are overwhelming. It is a major problem! Thanks to so many people taking action and speaking up, the need to focus more strongly and develop more effective forms of protection is now more obvious.

I've spent over five years of my life, dealing with finding information and educating myself about this disgraceful occurrence, and many others are speaking out about it. The information we've gathered will be used to contribute to our education services for creating more awareness, building community, and hopefully we will see changes in systems that lead to prevention. We are after all, along with many others, helping to identify a huge problem. Once people comprehend the extent of this issue, and more people become actively involved, with a genuine interest in actually following through and seeing better outcomes, we will all be part of a very large movement that helps to develop a system that protects elders.

These days, I certainly have regained my strength, and I'm enjoying a productive life. I now appreciate a high level of wellness and happiness. I need to feel well in order to embark on an awareness campaign such as this and do the work. Not only was I determined to build on my level of well-being and develop it, but at some point something kicked in as I regained my composure and sense of self-worth. That's when I said to myself, "They're not going to win!" The truth of the situation should be exposed, particularly the people who abuse elders for their money. Simply hearing about it is most upsetting, but you get past that and get on with the task at hand.

As mentioned previously, some of the tactics that the perpetrators use involve lying about and slandering the good reputations of decent people who have innocently been caring for elders. Doing this helps offenders achieve what they set out to do: get the money—and take someone's inheritance in the process. If you have experienced this, I suggest you consider doing the same as I chose to do. Resolve at this point to be firm and believe that your life is going to be a good life. Now I'm doing something about it that I consider to be of the utmost importance.

I knew I'd have to work on it, and it takes time, but I made the commitment for myself, for others who shouldn't have to endure this, and for their loved ones. They have to witness how these greedy, controlling, and manipulative people attempt to destroy someone they love by assassinating their good character, just so they can get control of assets and money. Someone I know who is quite an accomplished person was recently discussing how to structure a new organization. As we spoke of the people who carry out the ultimate betrayal, she said, "These are horrible people, Anne." I have to agree with her.

Some four years on, after finding out all this information and holding the many conversations and discussions, I become aware of feeling despair in their stories. It affected me quite negatively. But I can honestly say, I and my family do have a great life now. It's full of good people, and I can confidently say we enjoy it. We are mindful not to let the reckless people be part of our lives. I don't have time for people who make me feel less than I am, or for that matter people who think it's okay to put others down to feel better about themselves.

I most certainly do not have time for people who lie and do the wrong thing. To me, coercing, manipulating, and abusing elders for financial gain is a very low act. Perhaps that's the sort of people they really are; they only care about themselves, and they show no regard or consideration for other people, even though some of them pretend to for the sake of keeping up appearances.

The Truth of the Matter, and How It Goes Unnoticed

A Concept called Inheritance Impatience

> We can always depend on some people to make the best, instead of the worst, of whatever happens.
> —Sandra Wilde

As four years passed (slowly, it seemed), while gathering this information, I met so many people affected by senior wealth abuse. I also participated in countless conversations and meetings with professionals who are regularly exposed to it. It didn't make me feel good, and I decided if I was going to do this work, I would need to take care of myself to ensure I could carry it through with my well-being intact. I did take some time to have a brief break, to contemplate how everything could be coordinated effectively, and to reorganize my life and living arrangements. Now I am ready for action, and I'm in a much stronger position to move forward and actively embrace the task that lies ahead.

However, it did take considerable time to complete books and work up a plan, as well as complete some other projects in order to free up more time for me to participate to the extent that will be required. I was surprised at how long everything seemed to take, but I kept my eye on the end result and kept going. Focus and attention to detail is key. The amazing part of this process is that I didn't expect was to meet so many wonderful people along the way who would help. They offer ideas or assist in some way, or they simply give words of encouragement. Overall, they were very keen to see that we get this up and running. This did reinforce to me just how much people don't like the ultimate betrayal. Considering the response so far, approval for my project is the general consensus among most people.

On a personal note, for those who have been affected firsthand by the actions of the offenders who carry out wealth abuse, I've heard about how devastating or upsetting it can be. There is an underlying thread by those affected, and that is at some point they make a decision to cut offenders out of their lives and not let them back in. People sometimes make it known to others what the perpetrators have done. I have to admit, when I was absorbing all the information, I felt rather awful for a while with my recently gained knowledge about wealth abuse. It wasn't until one day much later, when it was a beautiful day outside, the weather was perfect, and I was thinking about how much better life is now, that something occurred to me.

It appears that for a lot of the people affected (including the ones who have lost part or all of their inheritance as a result), when they reach a certain point where they decide not to let the manipulators or wealth abusers upset them anymore, they begin to move on with their lives. I even noticed that with myself: I wasn't prepared to accept people in my life who were not of good character. Therefore, one reason for my life improving somewhat is that I did somehow manage to excommunicate all the people who were simply not well-meaning people. Today there's no room in my life for people who lie and do the wrong thing. There's only room for good people who, instead of dragging me down, make me feel good because they are decent human beings.

I was thinking about all this while driving to the post office. The underlying thing I noticed about senior wealth abuse, especially when it's carried out by family members, is that they usually don't care for those elders they've abused. They may say they do, however the money is far more important to them. They appear to operate on a totally different level compared to most genuine, caring people I've met. They can be deceptive in that they speak as though they care, but the reality is they don't. They care much more about themselves, and perhaps they really have no perception of how they are hurting people.

It's possibly worth considering that it's not the most appropriate choice to have this type of person assisting and helping elders. When you follow what happens during wealth abuse of elders, and you look at the trail of destruction of the family wealth abusers leave behind, not to mention the devastating states in which they leave elders and their loved ones, it truly is hard to comprehend. It's a major concern to those who know what these people do to elders, just to get at money. For those who've had to endure their tactics and the ramifications of their actions, they could be forgiven for saying something like "What have the idiots got the elder to do this time?" Sadly, I've heard of this type of situation all too often.

The stories are along the same lines, where elders had already been passively aggressively verbally abused to change their wills and sign other legal documents. Then the elders died, leaving practically everything to the people who were manipulating them at the time. I can't help but think that there must have been some big blowups in the families when one or two of them realized the others had outmaneuvered them and manipulated parents to leave most of the assets to them. While all this totally inappropriate behavior and conduct was being carried out, the elders were usually not aware they were being subjected to financial abuse. They should never have had to experience this.

You may be thinking by now that this story is a complicated one, and it often is. For some the experience can be brief and swift, but for others it can keep going for a very long time. It can go from bad to worse over many months. However, at some point while looking into it, it also occurred to me if I hadn't decided to say or do anything, and if I had not decided to take any action (and believe me I have taken a lot), what would have happened then? Would it have changed by itself? For legal reasons, I cannot give specific details of the abuse I've been told about. However, I can say that too many times I've heard of the devastation caused to an elder person who has been financially abused. The elders are obviously very upset, as they explain the details. Some describe how they did not take action simply because it was too difficult for them to deal with at their stage of life. They couldn't cope with it. Most often they were reluctant to do anything about it because they were too upset, humiliated, and ashamed family members were involved.

For some, it appears the shock of financial abuse being carried out by their own family members stopped them from taking any action. My point is, that the abuse of our elders could continue to go relatively unnoticed, if we choose not to take any action. We need to speak about this issue. There are others speaking up, writing articles, putting up blog posts, and doing interviews about it. That is most commendable, however overall it appears the voice and message needs to be stronger and louder, and more needs to be done if we are to address this issue of massive proportions. The real elephant in the room needs to be dealt with.

There's something to keep in mind if you think your parents have been abused or are possibly at risk: do look into it. Do something, even if it is simply becoming aware. If you don't—if you look the other way, not wanting to know—they could be abused in a far worse way than if you were to let your presence be known. Make it very clear to the abusers or possible abusers that you can and will take action if necessary. You can even mention the details of the law on undue influence, or have a plan in place as to what to do. You may find that doing the work and checking the legal details before anything happens is preferable. If you do, you could help the elders in your life avoid experiencing the destruction of family wealth and the degradation of their sense of well-being and safety.

You could consider making it obvious that you will do something to intervene, because you know the truth of the matter, and therefore you might just prevent it. At some stage you may find that the effort you put into gaining awareness and becoming informed was not in vain.

That's how I view it. The more people who know, the better we can help protect the elders. Even if it occurs in your family and assets are lost, if you step in and speak up, you may prevent further erosion of assets and exploitation of your elders. Maybe you're in the unfortunate position where financial abuse has already occurred, and perhaps the perpetrators turned the elders against you in order to access the assets. They may even have told lies to the elders. One day, the elders may find out the truth; they usually do know the truth of the matter but get caught up with the lies and manipulation.

Time really does help. Be patient, look after yourself, and work toward leading your best life. Keep any records you may have, because one day you may need to produce them. When something as horrible as financial abuse occurs to your dearly loved elders, and to you, remember that over time you do get back your strength and your enthusiasm for life. Even though you don't forget, you do get to a point where you can start to live your life again and enjoy the little things. It does take some time. Perhaps consider doing something that will assist you to deal with it. Embark on projects you enjoy. Walking is good too, and a good diet is always important. These days I try not to dwell on the negative things; the elders wouldn't want us to be upset by this. They would much rather see us move on and do something to create good lives for ourselves and for our families.

When you consider all the stories of what occurs during elder financial abuse, it is difficult to comprehend the full extent of it. However, if you've personally been affected, you've explored all avenues, and you find there appears to be nothing more you can do about it, I strongly suggest you consider being patient. There are some instances where, if the elder has not already passed on early due to the upset of financial abuse, in some cases the elder may find a way to reach out to you and make things right at a later time. In those situations, the elder may eventually see who is actually telling all the lies or taking advantage of him, and he may change the will back to include you again. The elder may overcome the obstacles and reach out to you, wanting to see you again. The elder may want to set things right if possible.

Of course, elders should not have been placed in this situation to begin with. Education, awareness, and prevention are the key overriding factors here. We all need to do whatever we can and play a part to see if we can collectively bring about more awareness and changes in this area. This appalling conduct has already upset many millions of elders and their loved ones. It can't be left for someone else to do. It can't wait until someone else is ready to do something about it later. The people who have done this should not be allowed to hurt any more elders!

I've had enough of hearing about the behavior of the unsavory characters who carry out abuse of the elderly for money. It has been very upsetting and draining—mentally, physically, emotionally, and financially. Yes, financially too. It costs a lot of money and time to get involved and get something like this up and running. However, the thought of this continuing to happen to older people drives me, and everyone I speak with, to do something about it. It's a sad fact that elder financial abuse is so devastating at the time, but unfortunately these older people are being manipulated, and often because of how it's carried out, there's not always a lot their loved ones can do to prove it legally and to help protect assets. Sometimes in trying to step in, people exhaust all the options, and there's nothing more they can do.

In some instances, those who try to step in are unsuccessful because it's not easy to compete with lies. Then they have to console themselves by saying something like "I did try. I tried everything I could possibly do, and it was a huge effort both emotionally and financially." When it first happens, if they do take action and are unsuccessful in getting a hearing or the assistance needed in order to take the appropriate legal course of action, the problem may be it was too difficult to prove at the time, even though there may have been consistently large withdrawals from the elder's bank accounts and other supporting documentation. At the time, some elders may not comprehend what is happening, and they may even believe all the lies they have been told. One day they'll know, but by then they may be concerned or worried because there may not be any money left.

At some stage, it usually becomes obvious, and the facts are fully realized. Then eventually other people find out the truth. I know my own dear father would be turning in his grave right now, because he wouldn't like this one bit! He didn't like lies or the people who told them. I still vividly recall him saying, "There'll be no lies told in this house!" He said it with such conviction because he knew at the time, someone in the room was lying. I always admired his conduct. He was one of the decent people in the world, quietly commanding respect because he treated others with respect. He was a gentle man with a kind nature, and he was an absolute pleasure to spend time with. If he was here today, he would encourage me and anyone else involved to continue to speak up and protect elders. He'd want us to prevent more elders from being financially abused. There is no way I'm going to ignore what is done to our elders.

One day as I was working in my office, writing and producing a body of work to help prevent elder financial abuse, something occurred to me. I paused and enjoyed the view outside, and I thought life in general had improved somewhat. Perhaps it was a good time for me to consider the hurt and what happens to the ones who are affected. Previously, I hadn't been as strong as I was now, but the knowledge of this actually motivated me. It compelled me to take action. I used that energy from my dislike for this abuse to give me the strength to take action. The thing I've noticed along the way is as you explain the details to people, they want to help or be supportive. Perhaps they were like me some years ago, quite unaware of the extent of this. Upon hearing of the facts, they actually encourage you. The fact is there are many decent human beings in the world who have this response, and they help to motivate you.

I hear of how the memories of elder financial abuse come flooding back to people when they speak of it. You can hear the deep hurt in their voices. Perhaps this wasn't the first time the elders changed their wills, or one of the elders they loved was verbally abused to sign legal documents. Then, you might hear of how after one of their parents passed on, the other was constantly harassed or manipulated. Yes, elders can be passively aggressively abused, sometimes daily, in order to change their will by another family member who wants it all. There can be one, two, or more people involved, jockeying for a position to get control of the money. They carry out their plan as soon as the right moment arises. One or more of them may decide to try to get it all even from each other! Make no mistake: if there's more that one involved, by all accounts they are in it together, and usually they have been from the start. They develop and initiate their plan quite cunningly to get control of the elder's assets.

Some elders, especially those who have had a difficult childhood or have limitations in some way, might go along with it all because they don't want any angst. The ones who take advantage of them can play on this, make them feel guilty, and keep at them every day, saying things like "If you really loved me, you would leave it all to me." Eventually the elder person might agree to make a new will. I can only imagine the upset in families or the fights that must occur when news of a changed will breaks out when decent people suddenly find they've been outmaneuvered or swindled. In fact, the perpetrators' antics leading up to this point could have been quite unbelievable, absurd, and nothing short of disgraceful. Some elders may be able to switch off to some degree, but they still should not have to go through this. In their later years, they deserve to be much more comfortable.

There may be elders who have lost capacity in some way, and initially when this first begins, they may sign any legal document put in front of them. You don't often know what they're told by the perpetrators. For this reason, there may be nothing else that can be done. On some level the elders may even find comfort and enjoy all the attention, not realizing what it actually means. That was the other hard thing about my research: hearing of people being unable to do anything else to prevent the further erosion of the elder's assets. In the end, the only thing people can do is to stay in contact with elders. As one lawyer said to me, "It is a good thing to stay in touch with the elders. They might find they need a lifeline".

There were similar and possibly complicated stories, such as when one of the elders was managing all the affairs, suddenly became ill, and experienced ongoing health difficulties. The other parent may have been presenting with symptoms of the onset of dementia, or was not of sound mind. It may not have been serious enough to have him or her assessed, because up until then the other elder with good capacity was quite capable of managing their affairs and may not have thought the competent elder would pass first. But if it happens, the outcome can be realized all too late, and the surviving elder may not have the financial skills or may not be of sound mind. In some instances, it could even be said the elder ignores the whole thing, sometimes reveling in all the attention; at times he or she may try to cover it all up, pretending it didn't happen, because it was too much to handle. Many elders don't fully understand, or if they do on some level, there will be many regrets when the truth starts to sink in, the money runs out, and the evidence becomes more apparent.

Are There Signs Beforehand?

Once people have been through something like this, they look back on that time and ask questions like "How did this happen, and why? Were there any signs?" There could be other questions, such as "What are the signs?" On reflection, you could hear them saying something like "I did notice certain things that started occurring a year or two earlier." Another might say, "I'm not sure—it just suddenly happened." People might talk about how certain people, in particular some family members, started to become slightly hostile toward them for no apparent reason. Another person might explain how a father or uncle preferred that he assist them with their living and financial arrangements, and that they stated this to their financial advisor, but that didn't deter the perpetrators.

This is not an uncommon arrangement, I know in my own life, when I was helping my parents, their financial advisor was fully aware I helped them to the extent I did. She knew this because I attended all the regular meetings with Dad, and she had records of all the meetings stating this. My parents' financial advisor was well qualified and was a good, caring person. We came to know her well, and we noticed how she was thorough and very respectful to her clients. That was probably why she was given the more senior clients' investment portfolios to look after. I still recall her words when I later explained what I was working on now and outlined the details. She sighed and then commented, "You know, Anne, you think that you do the right thing, and that your family members are brought up properly to do the right thing. Then they do this. It's terrible!"

I asked all the people I spoke with, "Were there any signs leading up to this happening?" I often heard comments such as "I suppose I overlooked it all, put it down to poor behavior, because I would not have behaved that way. I guess that's why I couldn't believe others would." Then some would add, "They were meant to be family. I had no idea what they were planning to do. I honestly thought they would never do something like this." Other comments were, "I was under the impression that family doesn't do things like that, and my mother always taught me to look after family members." The quote in chapter 1 is quite true even today, except in cases where the perpetrators do not wait until the parents have passed to dispute a will. They bowl straight in there and completely upset the lives of elderly people, some of whom have health problems. This concept is now being called "inheritance impatience".

As mentioned earlier, the people who plan to do this are usually very cunning and manipulative, and often they have been planning how they will do this for some time. It's still hard to believe that they actually plan to do this, and often they'll wait until the older people are more vulnerable. Sometimes it can take them a couple of years to implement their plan, but as soon as there is an opportunity, they go for it, and they don't seem to care who they hurt in the process.

Perpetrators can strike at a time when they have the best chance, such as when an elderly person has been diagnosed with a terminal illness. Perhaps elders become confused about financial details or the arrangements in their lives, or perhaps dementia begins to set in. In some cases, the ones who have basic or complex activity limitations lose their partners who have cared for them, leaving them vulnerable. Whatever the situation may be, as soon as aggressors see an opportunity, they launch their plan. Sometimes when the innocent people are so busy and carefully looking after the elders, taking them to see their doctors and specialists, they don't see it coming. They are not prepared, and for this reason they don't recognize the signs because they don't suspect it could happen. They certainly don't think anyone in his right mind would do such a thing.

But people do it, and they will pursue it. They'll take control of an elder person's wealth any way they can, and they'll lie and manipulate the situation until they succeed. They will even use defamatory behavior to help them remove the ones who might protect the elders, just so they can ultimately get control of the money and the house, eventually having it all for themselves. It's inconceivable that some people could be so cold and heartless, but unfortunately the prospect of getting their hands on the money seems to override any sense of discernment, responsibility, or respect.

To this day, I still can't fathom this type of behavior, let alone the fact that some people actually conspire to do this. During the past four years, while I've been compelled to gather information, it was like a snowball effect, and I would hear so many stories about this happening. It brought me to the realization that this is reaching epidemic proportions. People don't speak about it because often it's family, and they're upset and embarrassed. It's not spoken about, with perhaps the exception being to mention it to others who have experienced it. I've noticed when I bring up the subject in conversation, people then feel they can explain their stories, and they speak of how they were affected by wealth abuse.

The main ones who are affected are the ones targeted, and they are usually too frail or lacking in confidence by the time the abuse occurs to complain loud enough and to seek help. Plus, they're too embarrassed or hurt to say they were ripped off by a family member, a caregiver, a gardener, a neighbor, a new friend, or in some cases a supposedly trustworthy financial advisor. Consider how upsetting that must be for an older person: to have led a good and productive life, to have provided for your family and help them whenever you can—only to realize at the end of your life that they don't respect you or your demands, and they take your money any way they can. Imagine for a moment what that would feel like! Imagine it happening to you when you are older!

10

It's Their Money, and It's Their Whole Wealth

Having Money Should Be a Good Thing

She didn't make a million by inheriting it, she saved it.
—Helen Linhart

Even though it's the elders' money, it's not just about taking the money. If your money is taken, so is the freedom to live your life in your later years, in the way you choose. Living well—good food, good lifestyle, social activities, and travel, freedom to buy yourself personal items—costs money, and all of these things contribute to your well-being and freedom to enjoy yourself. Older people sometimes need even more money in their later years, if they need additional care at some stage. If the money is taken from them, so are their choices.

Some years ago, I recalled my still unanswered question: "Where did the obvious family wealth go, and what happened to all the money?" I'd already looked into my mother's family wealth, and I raised the question then. But more recently it was prompted after I received an e-mail from a distant uncle who lived overseas and was working on my father's family tree. When I looked into my father's family tree, I found that my father had an incredible history. They were people of commerce and generally did well. Some even had a small theatre company and entertained the royal children many generations earlier. On my mother's side, apparently a couple of generations back in Australia, her family was big property owners northwest of Sydney in the Hunter Valley. They were also quite involved in the Sydney social scene, were members of the best tennis clubs, and owned property in Sydney, in the exclusive area of Mosman.

It's a very interesting process to look into your family tree, take in the details, and then look at your own life. You might even find some correlations or connections. However, my point is that my parents' families had money, especially my mothers. So where did it go? There certainly is not any now. The family wealth had not been protected, and there was nothing left. As far as I could tell, it hadn't been maintained as a traditional family would have done.

The wealth my parents had accumulated in their lifetime was not huge; it had been built over the years, in particular by my father, who had worked very hard. Sometimes he held down two or three jobs just to make ends meet. He had worked tirelessly during all those earlier years to support us, and my parents were able to grow their wealth thanks to an astute property purchase. Dad managed to buy and keep a small acreage property when he returned from the war. He paid this off over time, and I believe he was offered a low-interest plan by the government, because he was a returned serviceman.

Back then, my father followed what turned out to be good advice from his mother. He bought the small acreage property. It needed a lot of work, and despite it being very difficult at times, he kept going. Eventually they owned it. My father didn't have a lot of cash money, however he did have an asset in the property, and in later years they were able to use this by selling it to purchase another property and invest some money. Fortunately for them both, their assets grew in value due to that good property purchase and those investments. When they retired, with some help from me and a good financial planner, they became financially comfortable. That money gave them the freedom they required to choose how they lived, without having to be concerned about the care they may require or being able to afford it in their later years.

Getting back to my point, I always wondered where the money had gone in both families, but especially in my mother's family, because by looking into the history, it was obvious how wealthy they were. Many people, they may get to this stage, look back at their families, and ask much the same thing. Perhaps it is time we consider how to protect the wealth in the family so that it will be there for the elders, because it's their money after all. However, in addition to this, if there's enough money or assets, this can be passed on to loved ones in a fair and just way. Ultimately, the family wealth is then maintained for future generations.

I recall watching a television interview with a retired registered nurse. She commented on how she made the transition from feeling absolutely awful to feeling rich, and how much better feeling rich is. She described it well. She was in a situation where the landlord of the house she was renting kept raising the rent, and she struggled to pay it; her own personal needs weren't meant as a result. When she made the choice to downsize and move to a lovely but smaller (and affordable) apartment, it freed up money for her to live and enjoy herself. Her comment was "Now I feel rich, and I'm doing this interview so I can tell others about it." It was obvious watching her enthusiasm just how much better she felt.

I know with my own life, things always came easily to me. I seemed to do with ease what many personal development people speak of today. I found it wasn't difficult to work toward something I wanted to have in my life, and it would unfold almost effortlessly. It happened easily because I followed my instincts while leading my life. Most important, I learned to pay attention to my intuition. I developed good radar, and I remembered to keep the focus on what I was working on while considering what was possible. Yes, it required diligence, putting in effort, and being patient sometimes. It worked well for me, and I've had a good life—and still do today.

Those I helped also had a good life, my parents included. In fact, I'd been helping them since I'd returned from working in New Zealand. When I first arrived back in Sydney, I noticed my parents seemed unhappy. They were going through the motions each day but not enjoying themselves. They had lost interest in their lives. I had the knowledge of how to create a good life for myself, and I began to ask my parents what they would like their life to be like. We would speak often, and they gradually became excited about what they wanted to do. They developed ideas, and we started looking at whether they would like to move and how they might like to live.

My role was not tell people what to do, but merely to facilitate and help them consider the possibilities. They chose for themselves, and I helped them bring it all together, like a project manager. We looked at how if they sold their property, which was run down but had high property value, they could afford to buy a really good home with half the money and invest the rest so they'd have money to live on and enjoy themselves. Their investments would grow as well and supplement their income, giving them plenty of money to enjoy their lives, yet they would still see their assets grow. They loved the idea, and with the knowledge they'd be able to have the lifestyle they wanted, I could see their level of happiness and enthusiasm start to grow. They realized they had choices, and they were able to choose how they wanted their lives to be.

We worked with a reputable financial adviser and set up a separate income stream for them once they sold their house. I remember Dad kindly saying at one stage, "When we sell the house, perhaps I can give my children some cash, an equal share each."

I pointed out, "Dad, that's very generous of you, but if you do that, you and Mum won't have any funds to invest, and you won't have that income stream to live on." They chose not to do that, and instead my parents arranged with their lawyer to have their wills drawn up, leaving any assets to their children in equal shares. That extra income stream they earned from their investments later gave them a wonderful life in retirement.

In fact, my parents enjoyed the process of moving immensely. Each week we met and looked at houses in different areas north of Sydney. We would have lunch and make a day of it, and they soon settled on an area west of Lake Macquarie. It was not far off the freeway, so friends and family could visit easily and often. The perfect house was soon found, and the look on Mother's face was one of pure joy. It was decorated with her favorite shade of blue, and it overlooked the water. It was a beautiful two-story home, was only seven years old, and was low maintenance. They could settle in two weeks because their acreage property had already sold, and the owners of the house had their other property and were in the process of moving. It happened so easily, and everything fell into place. They began to feel happy, and I could see it on their faces.

They had so much fun when they moved. For the first time in their lives, they went out and bought new furniture for the new house, as well as a late model car. They would go out for lunch; they didn't do that before, but they could now. It was such a delight to see how much they were enjoying themselves. For the first time in a very long while, they were able to make more choices and do things they wanted to do, because they weren't limited by lacking money. All of it was thanks to their newfound freedom, and for the first time they were financially in a good place.

I think that's one of the keys to enjoying your life: not having to worry about money. When you don't have to be concerned about how you're going to pay your bills, and when you know you can do the things in life that you want to do, the world around you can become much more enjoyable. You have the freedom to enjoy yourself without worrying about how to pay the bills and how you will cope when you're older.

For my mother, it was the house and the view she loved most, and she was very happy living there. For Dad, there was an unexpected bonus: the local RSL Club branch had numerous members who were returned servicemen. He easily made many friends there. They would often catch the train to Sydney, and my father was able to receive recognition for his contribution in the Korean War. He was a medic in the war and was initially based in Japan. He often spoke about Japan, and I think his time there was with good people. He had planned to go back there to marry, before he met my mother on his return.

For many years, Dad didn't speak of the war at all, but now he found a special group of friends through the club who helped him in many ways. He received his medals, commendation certificates, and a Gold Card, which entitled him to full medical coverage. With this, he knew as he aged, he would be well cared for. He could even receive full palliative care in his home, if ever it was needed. This later became very important to him because after many years of enjoying their new lifestyle, my father developed Parkinson's. It was the type where his movement decreased over time. It became painful and restrictive, but we managed very well, and he was very pleased with the nursing service that came to the house. The nurses were most pleasant, showed him respect, and were well trained and professional. I noticed they had a way of making Dad feel good during their regular visits.

When he was first diagnosed, Dad was invited to attend an eight-week course on Parkinson's, and he was allocated contacts at a special Parkinson's unit in the major hospital nearby, including a specialist Parkinson's registered nurse to contact if he had any queries. I took him to the course and participated; they put me in the category of his carer, so I was educated as well. Later I often contacted the nursing unit to consult on different things that would help Dad. It worked out very well for my father, and he felt supported and received the help he needed. The move proved to be ideal for both my parents. My father was the one who surprised me, though. He was a country person, but it turned out he loved the water too, and he gained great pleasure from walking along the waterfront reserve, watching the sparkling water and the different boats that moored there. He said he found it peaceful. The village-like area they settled in was called Wangi Wangi. The name was apparently an Aboriginal word, and we were told it meant "Place to Rest by the Water," or something similar to that.

Many years passed, and my parents were very happy with all their arrangements. I was concerned about them later; it was only natural as they aged, and I hoped they would be safe and secure and live the rest of their lives as happily as they could. For many years my parents' new house was filled with light. It had large windows to see the view, it was clean, and the water on the lake sparkled as one looked out. Whenever I visited, I felt happy there because my parents were happy, and I was made to feel welcome because my parents didn't have anything to worry about. They were good people, felt secure in their lifestyles, and were financially secure.

As mentioned earlier, I'd been assisting them for many years, along with their financial advisor, in order to grow their wealth. However, in the later years, it was more about maintaining it and not making things complicated for them. We would meet annually with the financial advisor, sometimes with phone calls in between meetings, just to make sure everything was in good order. My mother was involved for the first two appointments, but after that she lost interest in the investment details and preferred not to attend. She never did look at any of the paperwork; she trusted Dad and me to do that. When Mum stopped going to the appointments, Dad and I continued together. Perhaps he invited me to attend because he knew I had a good understanding of how everything was set up, and he trusted me.

Mum was perfectly content with receiving her generous allowance each month. It was my mother who had asked for a large allowance in the initial planning meetings, and even though the financial advisor was rather surprised and queried it, because it was a high amount, Dad said it was okay. He always looked after her well. A generous allowance meant Mum could easily afford quality health supplements and health care, and she had some spending money to buy gifts for family and friends, and for all her craft projects. They had sufficient funds to last them and still leave an inheritance to their children. An inheritance was important to them, to be equally divided among their children.

I recall my father telling me when he was speaking to his lawyer while they were preparing their wills, Dad said to him, "Divide the inheritance into equal shares. You always have to treat them the same." He said this with a proud smile on his face.

One day I remember saying to my parents when we were in the kitchen, "Look how far you've both come. You have a lovely home, a good lifestyle, and good health. Well done. You should be proud of what you've achieved." They stood there in the kitchen that day with very pleased smiles on their faces, and I was so proud of them both. Yes, I helped them often when they needed it, but that was my gift to them because I loved them. They were my parents, after all, and they were good people. They made their own choices, and they chose what they wanted to have in their lives.

They owned a beautiful waterfront reserve home and had enough cash invested to last them a lifetime. They had nothing to worry about, and if anything needed to be done, they'd ring me and it was done. They could afford a part-time cleaner—someone to tidy the lawns, tend to the garden, and wash the windows. They even decided to install a lift chair so they could stay in their house in their later years, following a consult with their occupational health professional. We always consulted with their health care providers. I merely helped them facilitate their life choices; it was about what they wanted and how they wanted things to be. They were enjoying their lives. I felt good when I visited them because they felt safe and secure in the knowledge that all was well.

They had prepared their wills and legal documents, consulted with their lawyer, and retired with a good health management plan in place. They loved where they lived and looked into all the important details of their lives with their advisors. Everything was in order. Basically, their wills were identical and stated that in the event of my parents passing, the assets were to be evenly divided between their children. I was appointed the executor of their wills. Both my parents specifically stated that they wanted me to be the executor in their lawyer's office, and I signed, accepting to be the executor. They followed the advice of their financial people and their lawyer.

Many people do the same thing as my parents. They think they have done all the right things, and then somehow the perpetrators still manage to raid the assets. There are many people out there doing the right thing, following all the appropriate courses of action, and being good and caring people. But unfortunately, sometimes it's not enough to protect them in their later years. It becomes obvious that there is a need for setting boundaries. Just how one does this is the big question.

11

Other Insights about the Gray Area

The Idea of a Register

A couple of years after my father passed, I was already looking into the issue of wealth abuse among elders. Someone made a remark that I thought summed it up quite well. It was one day when I'd first started writing this book, and a consultant employed by our telephone service provider called. He was organizing our new phone plan, and while doing this, he asked about the nature of the book I was writing. His words have always stuck with me; it was a basic but straight to the point way to describe it. He was a worldly sounding man, and when I explained the book's subject matter, his comment was "Yes, I've seen it. Suddenly when people reach this stage in their lives, and they're elderly, other people around them seem to become obsessed with getting at their money, and they behave like crazed animals!"

Those words stayed with me, and when I thought about it more and remembered people's stories, I thought that was quite an accurate comment. Perpetrators think they can do whatever they please and abuse elders for financial gain. In some cases they might even move into the house uninvited. They tell elders what to do, they tell them lies, and often order them to sign legal documents. They will even lie in a tribunal or court hearing,

They may even state that an innocent person who was helping the elders was behaving badly or inappropriately, was harassing the family, or had mental health issues. The extent of their lies is quite atrocious.

The lies they tell can have a detrimental effect on the outcome. It's a good idea to be prepared for it, if you are trying to step in and help elders in these situations. They could even lie and attempt to take legal action against you so that it appears you are the one who is causing a problem. There can be so many twists and turns in a court hearing, especially if perpetrators lie and manipulate others to lie as well. Do be prepared for that, and get as much proof as you can to back you up, because it can be difficult dealing with the type of person who will not only tell lies frequently but lie in a hearing as well.

In some situations, the people who abuse the elders in this way are not averse to creating scenes in front of the elders by making wrongful accusations against the people who are genuinely trying to protect them. All this is done to create diversions and drive away the good, innocent people. Often these decent people will go away temporarily because they don't want to cause any more aggravation for the elders. They have far too much respect for the elders' state of mind to upset them even further by participating in arguments in front of the elders.

If these innocent people have difficulty proving what they know to be true, it can be quite devastating for not only them but the elders too. They may not be able to spend their last Christmas with them, like they had so enjoyed for so many years before. In some cases, every time they try to visit the elders, the perpetrators create such a huge scene about the things they have supposedly done—which of course are lies—but those lies and the way they create these scenes are so upsetting for the elders that any good person will not choose to participate for fear of upsetting the elders even further. These are the tactics perpetrators use all too often. Sadly, it's commonly used as a means to take over the lives of the elders and access their wealth.

Christmas can be ruined, families are broken, and elders and their loved ones are left upset. Those hoping to spend a couple of hours with their elder parents or friends, whom they've easily visited many times before, are shut out. Yes, they are literally shut out of the house. Perpetrators can say the elders don't want to see them anymore, or that they don't want to take tablets anymore, or that they're resting the family can't see them. All the while, the elder is in the house, lying in bed or sitting in another room, cut off from those they once trusted so implicitly. Sometimes elders are unaware of what's about to occur, and sometimes they know exactly what is going on but are powerless to stop it. Even if perpetrators allow decent people into the house, they stay in the room or stand near the elder person, to ensure none of the details of wealth abuse are communicated. When there's more than one perpetrator, it makes it even harder to step in. As one person in the legal profession said to me with a look of distaste on his face during one of our meetings, "It's happening all over the place."

Sometimes perpetrators lie convincingly enough to take a court order against the innocent people trying to protect the elders. One lawyer whom I spoke with regarding these particular tactics and the use of charges brought to court stated firmly, "The law needs to be changed to prevent this sort of vindictive behavior from happening." Apparently anyone can walk into a police station, lie, and have one of these orders taken out against another person. The lawyer then mentioned some hard facts about the town when he said, "Half the town at any one time is taking out these apprehended violence orders, just to be nasty to someone. Most of these are a waste of taxpayers' money!" It's not exactly a good neighborhood that he works in; part of it is world renowned as a beautiful area, but there is another part that has a history of drug abuse and a high crime rate.

An important point to note is that elder wealth abuse doesn't just happen in any particular type of neighborhood. It's indiscriminate and can happen to the wealthy and not so wealthy, in any type of neighborhood. There is not one particular type of socioeconomic group where it occurs; it happens across the board.

In Australia, the term AVO is used for an apprehended violence order; it could have a different term in the United States or in other countries. I have many friends in the United States and have had conversations with them about this topic. The abuse of the elderly still occurs in the United States and other parts of the world, just as it does here. It's a problem in most countries throughout the world. One lady I spoke with in the United States told me of a story where, unbeknown to her, someone in the family moved in with an older uncle and prevented him from communicating with other family members. The perpetrator convinced this uncle to sign legal documents that gave her access to his money. Sadly this uncle didn't get to say good-bye to the people he loved. When the lady realized later what had happened, she managed to take this person to court afterward, and the perpetrator who did this to her uncle was made to pay back the money she'd taken by a court order.

The Aftermath: The Truth Comes Out Eventually

After some time of looking at all the information and considering all that happens during and as a result of the ultimate betrayal, plus the effects, I recall clearly how I felt. By knowing about this now, I seemed to move through different stages of emotions. At first the enormity and the absurdity of what occurs rendered me speechless. I was without words, but inside it felt quite soul destroying in a way. I took some time out in the fresh air and had a little break from everything. When I began to feel better, I recall walking up to my house, and I started to feel most annoyed about it all!

Perhaps those feelings of annoyance somehow turned into the motivation to take some steps into looking at what could be done to prevent this. I wanted to help prevent elders from being betrayed by perpetrators in their lives. At that time it came to me: I wasn't going to let what the perpetrators did, plus the knowledge of this issue, ruin my life! Instead, hopefully the insight I gained could be used to raise awareness and help prevent it. Admittedly it did take a while to regain my composure and strength after hearing about the consequences: the hurting of innocent people, the destruction of people's lives, and the trail of degradation and lost family wealth left behind as a result. I gradually became stronger and calmer.

I was fortunate to have some special people in my life: lovely friends who would quietly encourage me to continue, and my lovely daughter and husband, who gave me two very good reasons to be strong, take the high road, and look to change things for a better life—for us, for the elderly, and for future generations of families. For those affected directly by such a big and devastating turn of events, hopefully the knowledge that something is being done will help.

The main thing is to try to move on from it. How you do that is an individual thing, and in some cases it may take some time. The fact someone dear to you was a victim of elder financial abuse is a hard call for anyone, but you must find a way to lead your life and move on after that. Time helps, as does thinking of the good people who are in your life now and choosing not to let this low behavior win over your happiness and enjoyment of life. Know it may take some time, but there are so many good people in the world that you could have in your life. Decide not to associate with people who do these undesirable things to the elderly. Remember, too, that your elders would not want you to be upset.

Many months later, I thought, "Well, if there's nothing I can do immediately about this situation, then perhaps I can over time. I can help to educate others to assist them and hopefully head off this type of dysfunctional behavior in their own lives. If it saves more elderly people experiencing the same disrespect that other elders have, then that would at least be something worthwhile." To be able to do something to contribute to making this world a better place to live is a far more appealing and a better approach, a more desirable concept, and hopefully in the long term the outcome will be favorable for all concerned.

Immediately following the realization of the extent of wealth abuse, my husband and I decided to consult and meet with our own personal lawyer to ensure this type of situation could not happen to us or to our daughter later on. If these people who carry out this despicable act against elders are not easy to detect beforehand, then we wanted to be prepared to prevent it. That was what prompted us to ensure our wills were tight, to ensure the people bequeathed to in our wills actually received their inheritance. We ensured the family's whole wealth stayed intact with integrity.

That is the first step, arranging to have your will in place, and it's of course an important one. It's supposed to ensure that an inheritance is left for your loved ones—the ones you actually want to receive it. But there is obviously more to be done to protect people for when they become older. There perhaps needs to be something else to prevent the ultimate betrayal. It may be a couple of things that could be done. The solution is not totally clear, but surely there must be something. This is why at this point I'm preparing to facilitate extended workshops on the subject, because if people are more aware of the pitfalls, they can take measures to ensure seniors are safe and secure in their later years.

Today, instead of feeling there's nothing else I can do, I can at least do something to help. Just the other day, I had an appointment with a health professional. He is aware of what happens because I'd explained on a previous occasion the details of what occurs. Now, I was able to say to him recently, "If you have people who come to you upset because elders in their lives are being subjected to financial abuse, you can suggest they go to our website to become familiar with what happens."

He simply said, "Is this about asset protection, or is this about stopping the bastards who do this?"

I replied, "It's about both, really. It's about helping protect elders and what we call their whole wealth—their integrity and their quality of life."

As the appointment concluded, he enthusiastically said, "This is good, and I'm going straight to my computer now to look up the website."

That night when speaking with my husband, I mentioned this conversation with our health practitioner. I said to him, "So you see, the good people in the world don't like this. They don't like what happens to a lot of elders—not one bit!" People generally do not like this, and if more people were informed about it, there could quite possibly be more done to help prevent financial abuse of our elder seniors. Certainly awareness is key, and that is high on the priority list. Having the knowledge of how things work around this issue is so important.

Adding to the vitally important awareness and the general consensus among most people, there could be another vitally important tool to consider for the priority list: utilizing a register to assist us in our efforts to prevent wealth abuse. When I was speaking with a lawyer I know about what happens, he said, "I know it's not good, and it's happening all over the place. It's terrible, really." Later in that meeting, when I described my plans to do this work, he said "Good on you, Anne, for doing it."

Then I mentioned to him how, when having a recent conversation with my husband while we were proofreading the guide, I commented, "Am I the only one getting this? The fact this can be done to elders? That the wealth abusers can get a lawyer who doesn't know the older person and have new legal documents drawn up in their favor? Shouldn't there be some sort of register?" That was one of those lightbulb moments. It's not my area of expertise, however could one central register be set up (or something similar), with a level of security so that when seniors have their legal documents drawn up with their lawyers before they become elderly or vulnerable, it could be recorded and can easily be referred to and checked? He thought that was a good idea.

12

Maintaining Seniors' Wealth and Protecting Their Whole Wealth

It's Time We All Say No!

Creating wealth isn't just about having enough money. It's a whole mind-set, including a range of different areas of your life that come together, creating a beautiful life for yourself and for those you care about. It's a wonderful way to live one's life, and once people becomes aware of how to create whole wealth, then everything around them improves and keeps improving. That's how you move through your life, creating it as you go along and having plenty of money to do what you'd like to you. You can then make choices, and you have freedom in your lifestyle. By the time people are seniors, most of them have figured this out, and they can enjoy the later stage of their lives.

This is what seniors strive for, and they work all their lives to reach the point where they can enjoy this freedom, either in their later years or when they retire. Quite frankly, they should be able to enjoy all of it. They certainly have worked hard enough for it; they have put in their time, worked hard, looked after their family, saved money, and were good citizens in their community. No one has the right to come along, take their money, and ruin their lives. It's their money! By the time seniors reach this age, they usually have mastered how to live a happy life. They are not as worried about the little things anymore because they're generally in a good place financially. They've reached that stage where they are more educated and comfortable.

After hearing about what happens to elders as a result of wealth abuse, it prompted me to look at my own life. I became resolved to not let the knowledge of this ruin my life or my family. Afterward, when I regained my strength and recovered from how uncomfortable it made me feel, I made a decision to create a life even better than before. I decided at some point that what those horrible people do is not going to ruin my life. The elders wouldn't want that to happen. Now, I'm going to use that knowledge, do something important with it, and look into creating an awareness campaign to help prevent it. Setting up a think tank could even help to come up with solutions; that could be item number three for consideration on the high priority list.

I spent two years researching the topic of creating money and wealth for living in today's world by asking, "What are they teaching today?" To my amazement, I found that it's not dissimilar to what I had been doing myself. Even though I admit there is some room for improvement, the basic principle is the same. The thought did come to mind that perhaps if we could teach the unsavory characters who abuse the elders for their money how to create their own wealth, it could be part of the solution. Would there be less manipulation of our senior people, resulting in less of the abusers trying to access their money? However, there would still be greedy people who go after the money anyway, even if they already have wealth.

One new thing I learned was that when something happens that upsets you, don't let it ruin you or your life. Instead, use the energy of how it makes you feel to propel you toward the good things you want for your life. Those things can be more money, better finances, being happy, being safe, having good friendships, and maintaining relationships with your loved ones. This was something new for me, and I personally found it worked. This is a big key to being successful in your life, and to not giving up. Don't give up—keep going!

Your whole wealth, and also helping to create it for the seniors or elders you may be helping, is firstly about your physical health. Then you must work on the way you feel about everything: not worrying, how your house feels, is your business prosperous, your work, whether your finances are supporting you well, whether you have good people around you who make you feel good. Do you laugh or feel you're enjoying yourself? It all contributes to how you are able to enjoy your life and feel safe and secure.

Some people have money and don't feel any enjoyment at all, but that can be changed if they want it to. Some people don't have money and would love some more. Others have poor health, and by improving this, they can become happier and feel more content. The latter certainly is preferable to most people.

It's a process, a matter of deciding what you want to do and looking after yourself. Taking care of yourself is very important. Then you should keep the focus on the things you are working toward; don't let go, and don't give up. You are improving your life, and that's important not only for you but for your loved ones. If you're well and happy, you lift them up as well. It can take some time, so patience is key, but you do gradually get there.

Your whole wealth is also related to your level of intuition and learning to trust it; it is your internal navigation system. When you are actually doing this, you will notice how things get better, and money comes your way when you start to become a better money manager. You take responsibility for it, and your enjoyment level of your life increases. You make good choices and find it easier to be more positive. Good people come into your life, and some help you in small or big ways.

I recall how my father used to often say, "Go with the flow." I think he was talking about acknowledging your own good judgment and doing what feels right for you. When you are making good choices, things seem to work out better. He was a wise man, and I always felt good being around him because this was how he led his life. He was a good example of a decent human being, a good role model who helped others when he could. One thing I will say is that he preferred to keep foolish, reckless, and disrespectful people at a distance.

Unfortunately for some seniors and elders, there are certain people who can get close and are jealous and unhappy with their own lives. They may be envious of you, and they may not like the fact that you're close with the elders. They may even hate that you have such a good relationship, plus the fact that the elders trust you implicitly. To be blunt, after hearing of this, I often ask, "Is it simply that they are jealous, or do they want access to the wealth?" They most likely won't show how they really feel, and they conceal it well. But after the wealth abuse occurs, most decent people find themselves wishing that they'd known of this beforehand.

If it does happen in your life, and if you're feeling anger or remorse about the abuse of your elders, try to do something constructive. Let it compel you rather than devastate you, and see what you can do for yourself and for them. Don't doubt yourself or feel too guilty, and remind yourself that you are not the one who did this to them toward the end of their lives. Simply put, when the perpetrators want money, they'll go to great lengths to get it. They'll even stab you in the back just so they can take it, and they will take it any way they can.

This leads me to another important point, and that is having good people with good intentions close to you. Have you ever spent some time with someone, and when you walked away, you didn't feel good? Perhaps the words they used or their negativity stuck with you afterward. In contrast, have you ever been around someone and noticed how you felt good? The person's energy was light, and you felt lifted by being around him or her. That's the difference. Choose to be around the people around whom you feel good. If you get a bad feeling about someone or a situation, it's usually for a reason.

I recall listening to an interview that really struck a chord with me; it also complemented wise and knowledgeable things I'd heard previously. We not only incorporate things in our lives, but we help our parents to do this as well. I thought, "Oh, yes, that's what we created for my parents. That's why it was so good, and we did it almost on autopilot, always with good intentions." What we helped my parents to enjoy was much the same as what was mentioned in this interview about the seven keys to whole wealth. The seven levels are health, home, knowledge, purpose, presence, and truth. That was what we had, and it was a beautiful time in our lives.

In all honesty, although I enjoyed helping my parents and being around them, I don't think I fully appreciated just what a lovely time it was. When I was first compelled to look into the issue of elder financial abuse about five years ago, it certainly did make me appreciate that time more. It's hard to become involved and hear the stories of how wealth abuse happens to elders, especially when I've had good relationships with elders and understand how they can become frail and vulnerable in their later years.

Maintaining Seniors' Wealth and Protecting Their Whole Wealth

Protecting your whole wealth is about protecting your health, your money or assets, your well-being, your way of life, and your loved ones. A very good accountant I know, who now has her elder mother living with her, mentioned that by the time people become elder citizens, they like their finances and their investments to be kept simple so that they can easily see at a glance where it is and how much is actually there in their accounts. I thought that sounded like good advice.

Helping to improve or maintain a senior person's health is an important aspect of whole wealth, and it can be one of the easier areas to manage compared to protecting financial wealth. A senior person's level of wellness contributes to how he actually feels. Keeping your health in good order is crucial to your enjoyment in life. Eating well, having a healthy diet, and having healthy cells as a result is important in that it helps to prevent and fight off illness. It's common knowledge that plenty of green leafy vegetables contribute to the feeling of well-being. A good diet transfers to your level of energy and how good you feel; it can play a big part in how you conduct your life. The same applies for your business or work, if you're still working. The truth is, it's fundamental to how good you feel, and it's all interrelated. We can help our elders with this, as well as ourselves.

Unfortunately, many senior citizens' diets gradually deteriorate as they get older. If we can ensure they receive good nutrition, it contributes to the overall enjoyment of their lives and how good they feel. In my parents' case, I was close with them and knew what was happening. We ordered their meals and groceries for them, as well as helped them pay their bills and check on their finances. However, for the elders who have people with bad intentions taking over their affairs, this may not be the case. Perpetrators may not leave the elders', even if asked to do so, and they may be telling them a lot of lies about their financial arrangements and about the people who once helped them. They also may or may not be treating them with the respect they deserve. For this reason, it is wise to step in promptly when you can.

In order to do this effectively, you may be required to obtain a medical letter. All the letter might have to say is you are concerned because of the elder person's frail health or state of mind, and you worry they could be easily taken advantage of. Your lawyer will be able to advise you on the wording. If you manage to get such a medical letter, you can possibly head off a ruthless takeover of the elders' affairs, including their finances. The tribunals are aware of how difficult these letters can sometimes be to acquire, but they will help you as much as they can. Perhaps there needs to be more education across the board in this area.

My parents had their wills in place, and we thought we had everything in order, as did my husband and I with our own personal affairs. It turns out we actually did do everything correctly. A friend who is a family counselor said he always advises his clients that they choose their most trusted child to be the executor and have power of attorney. My parents prepared their wills with me as executor almost twenty years ago, and I had power of attorney if ever needed. They did all of this well before they reached their elder years, while they were still relatively young seniors, and when they were stronger mentally and physically. We didn't know about the ultimate betrayal and the triple-whammy effect. I naively presumed it was committed by ones with criminal tendencies or the obvious dubious people. But apparently perpetrators are not so easily detected.

Some unprepared people learn about it the hard way. There needs to be more awareness and more education. I heard people say along the way, while trying to step in, that the law doesn't protect elders. We now know there is a law, but it's often difficult to prove financial elder abuse. If this is the case, there must surely be changes we can make to improve the situation. Creating more awareness may be the key here, however we will also need to devise some solutions and take certain actions with careful consideration.

For some people, if you're looking to ensure your affairs are in order, it's certainly an important step to visit your lawyer and have your wills drawn up, preferably before you reach the elder stage of your life. Many elders occasionally check with their lawyers to make sure their wills are still current and cover everything they want. Some people decide that their children will be bequeathed an equal share of all their assets when they pass. Everyone's will varies depending on the circumstances, and that should be enough. However, if the ultimate betrayal comes into play, it's a whole different ball game.

The ultimate betrayal concerns what is occurring quite prevalently in our society; whether or not the elderly have a lot of money, it's still happening. When people become more elderly and frail, they're in the later stages of their lives. Unfortunately, the thought of getting money turns some people into disrespectful predators. They start to consider how to get the money for themselves, or a larger share of the money. The sad thing is they don't seem to stop to consider that there's an older person's self-respect at stake. They don't stop to consider that their actions are going to hurt someone in a big way. In some cases, they even cause elders to pass earlier than they would have normally because they've lost their whole wealth in the end, including their dignity.

That wealth, which of course belongs to those elders, has taken them a lifetime to accumulate. By this time they have a plan they're happy with, and that is to take care of them in their later years and to pass on some of that wealth to their loved ones as they choose. That's their right to choose—until the ultimate betrayal occurs, and then that right is ignored. Elders usually don't see it coming, because the people who do this are cunning and sneaky, and they have a plan. They don't care about anything else and are determined to get the money and assets. They will stop at nothing, and they will lie, scheme, forge signatures, and even abuse elders into signing legal documents.

It's Time We All Say No!

It's a disgrace that elder wealth abuse happens at all today, but it does. Some say the law doesn't protect the elderly or the frail enough, because in these cases it's difficult to prove abuse, which does nothing to help the matter. That's what I was told when initially consulting with a lawyer: "The law doesn't protect the older people from this happening." He wasn't knocking the system or the law, but rather making an honest comment considering all the usual surrounding circumstances. As I found out after looking into everything, in some cases it's straightforward, but in others it can be a minefield.

Furthermore, it can be extremely difficult for the older people if they become the target of wealth abuse. They could be waiting— for what must seem like a very long time—for someone they trust to get legal assistance and step in. If that doesn't work, and elders are left in that situation, they're often devastated. In some cases, everything a person does to take action and to look for legal assistance to step in is headed off by the perpetrators. A lawyer I spoke with recently is proposing a new law called the elder justice law – that could be one of the solutions.

Sometimes it appears medical people are too afraid or too cautious to speak up or get involved. They may be afraid of getting sued, or they are not actually sure of the circumstances, and so they put it down to a family dispute. However, in the cases where the ultimate betrayal is occurring, it's modern-day piracy. When some are advised initially that there's not a lot they can do, I suggest they at least try to see if something can be done.

There was one story where the people said, "We have to try!" For three months, every day, they left no stone unturned. They contacted numerous professionals and organizations. In the end, they couldn't get any action, and this resulted in them being unable to step in. To their dismay, they could not assist the elder. These once trusted helpers were rendered powerless to step in and help return that elder's house and finances. They failed in returning that elder person's right to be able to make his own choices. That right was taken away from the elder without his consent. Isn't it about time we changed things?

I recall when a good friend found out what happens to these elders. He said to me, "This type of abuse of the elderly for their money is one of the worst forms of abuse." Our beautiful older people deserve to be treated with respect. I love being around older people. By the time they've reached this age, they don't have a lot of time for people who are being silly; they're straight to the point and tell you to your face what's on their mind. I like people like that. Their sense of humor is usually very good by then too, and they're fun to be around.

Let's do something about it. Let's not stand for it anymore, and see whether we can change some things to make it a better experience for our seniors. Our elderly people should not have to experience this. In many cases they have helped us get where we are today. One day we will be older too. I know I certainly want to know my later years will be comfortable, with my dignity still intact, and I want the same for my child and grandchildren later.

For People in the Legal Profession

The lawyers I've met in the course of learning about the ultimate betrayal are honorable, hard-working, professional people, and they're good at what they do. They help people very well with their legal matters. However, you may have heard the saying, "There are some, and then there are some others." I haven't met the "some others" in the legal profession, but there is apparently a minority of lawyers who either wittingly or unwittingly help perpetrators carry out their underhanded plans. To be honest, they may have been lied to, and perhaps not all lawyers are aware of the extent of elder financial abuse. They don't stop to question the circumstances, therefore placing the older person at risk of being abused further.

However, it may be necessary to consider everything, ask more questions, and check further to see if there are legal documents already in place. The lawyers I know would most certainly do this and be thorough about it. They are highly trained and can tell whether someone's lying simply by looking at the person in the eye and observing body language. Their gut instinct is highly attuned because they have developed it over time and have learned to trust it. With regard to the lawyers who could assist the wealth abusers inadvertently, I say: please, before you just do the work and take the payment for it, look into it further! You may just find your client, or the person who has suddenly taken over an elder's affairs, is an elder financial abuser and is planning to carry out an unlawful act.

The lawyers I know would hold a conversation in private with the elders, or they might state, "I feel there should be an assessment of this elder person, because he or she seems confused." They might also firmly mention that it's against the law to manipulate and persuade an elderly person who has lost capacity to sign legal documents. That may be enough to stop the financial abusers, but it may not be. The abusers may find another lawyer who won't be so discerning. The lawyers need to be very careful they are not compromised, or else they may find that through no fault of their own, they have assisted someone who has now done something illegal.

By now you might be thinking, "Shouldn't there be a register of some sort that lawyers could check? Perhaps a central register, or some other way they could check to see whether legal documents are already in place for a senior or elder person?" A register could help enormously, for both the legal profession and their elder clients.

For Our Seniors Citizens—and Us, Eventually

As you can imagine, this type of betrayal is widespread and varies considerably. I certainly wish that I'd been more informed about the prevalence of this occurring in our society. If I had, I may have approached the conversation with my father at an early stage, before he became older and frail. He probably would have thought there wasn't any need to do that—I know I didn't, because I hadn't heard of it that much. Families are supposed to look out for each other. I know family is important to me.

If this has already happened to you or your elders, I suggest you consider not placing the blame on yourself. Instead, know that some people are simply not nice. It becomes obvious that when it comes to accessing money, some turn into horrible people and become quite capable of unpleasant conduct. We would like to think that everyone has a good character, but the fact remains some people turn very unpleasant when it comes to getting their hands on money. It doesn't worry them one bit that they crush a beautiful elderly person's dignity and self-esteem in the process of getting money or assets. I find the whole scenario very disappointing and a sad demonstration of the inhumanity of humanity.

If for some reason you are doubting the concept and the stories I'm writing about, or if you know of these dubious characters I'm talking about who have committed the ultimate betrayal, then I say to you emphatically, "Ask them to prove to you where the elder's money is!" Make sure they physically show you the paperwork and in detail. They are very good at lying, manipulating situations, and taking advantage of vulnerable people and their circumstances. Ask them to show you the paper trail and the bank account balances as proof, and there will be your answer. They won't be able to because either there isn't any money left, or they have transferred it to other bank accounts. You may well find money has been taken or lost somehow and is not in the elder's bank account, where it should be. As one person said to me, "The proof is in the bank accounts."

In the event this has already happened to you or in your family, keep the paperwork, because one day the truth may come out, and you'll be glad you did. You may have been advised that there's nothing else you can do by your legal people at this stage, and that you can dispute the will later when the parent passes. If you can, consider how you might stay in touch with that elder, because one day in the near future, the elder may need a lifeline. By the way, when I heard of how this was suggested sometimes—that you can always dispute the will—I said most emphatically, "That's not the point. The point is a decent elderly person has been abused!" I've mentioned what happens to people, and one comment was "Oh, that's terrible. Abusing an older person to sign legal documents is bad enough, but to take money out of their banks? That's just not right." I appreciate they're probably shocked by the explanation of what happens to the elders, but to me there's still something a little odd with that comment. Was taking the money worse than abusing the person? I'm sorry, but are we missing something here? Abusing one of our senior people, who may have helped built our lives for us, has to be one of the lowest forms of human behavior.

Taking their money is a huge issue, but abusing elders in order to do so is an even bigger offense. That's probably what those good people who made the comments meant after all. However, you may feel the same way, or you've experienced this too and feel upset that some people will lie about your good character. The fact is perpetrators will make defamatory comments about you, and they'll even embark on a campaign to destroy your good reputation with other people and with the parents or older relatives with whom you've shared such a wonderful relationship. Don't let them win. Don't let them crush your self-worth. There are still things that can be done. First, work on healing yourself and getting strong again. You can even join this campaign if you want to; be part of the new movement of people who will not stand for this anymore.

Something people can do to help is to talk with politicians at all levels. Write a letter to your local or federal member of parliament to help to create more awareness. The more letters they receive, the more they will take notice. Many people simply are not aware of the extent to which this occurs. I think that politicians generally want to help their communities, and they want to represent them well in parliament. If more people take a stand and say no to this low form of behavior, we can bring about change in this area. It has been my experience that politicians seem to be more than happy to find a cause and run with it, if enough people express their concern about it. It looks good for them to do this. They want to; that's their job. Don't be afraid to find your voice and speak up.

If you have lost an elderly parent or loved one to this form of abuse, there are things you can do to help create more awareness and to help prevent this from happening to other older people.

Ultimately, your efforts will make the world a better place. Wouldn't it be a wonderful thing if another book could be published in a few years about how much progress we've made in this area? We could celebrate that and even hold a campaign party to happily acknowledge how the decent people of the world can work together to bring about change and do the right thing! Then we could see how we've all done something truly amazing and have contributed to taking some action that is just and fair, for sake of the rapidly growing numbers of our senior citizens.

Acknowledgments

I would like to give a big thank-you to certain members of my own family, as well as to friends, trusted advisers and associates who have been such a huge help and are supportive in many respects. Appearing not in any particular order, they are: my wonderful daughter, Cate; my husband, John Arthur; Kathryn McPeake; Liane Harris-Moffat; James Kelly; Richard Mitry; Deborah Kuras; Jason Reynolds; Janet Foster Desdier; Linda Daniel; Tim Southwell-Keely; Christopher Kay; Michael Johnsen; Paul Fitz-Patrick; Rodney Lewis; Phillippa Sutton; Brian Moore; Michelle Clark; Heather Perry; Maurice Broaddus; and everyone at Archway Publishing. There were many others, too many to include here, who have offered kind and motivating words of support; they know who they are. As we progress, there will most likely be many more who will gladly assist in some way, if they can.

At some stage in the future, it would be a great pleasure to write another book that speaks about how things have changed, and about how people are more aware of elder financial abuse, resulting in the unlawful act being less likely to occur. Thank you in advance to everyone who will play a role in that occurring.

ABOUT THE AUTHOR

Anne is an advocate for elders. She believes people, especially elder people, should be shown the respect they deserve. Today, Anne is very much involved in looking at ways things can change for the better by creating more awareness. This awareness not only will lead to looking at ways to improve the care of elders in terms of financial abuse prevention measures, but it will also bring about changes in setting new guidelines to follow. Ultimately, society should assist elders to ensure their lifestyles and elder care remain intact in their later years.

After developing an interest in the field of public relations some thirty years ago and studying it for several years, Anne became a qualified professional public relations consultant. She successfully worked long-term with high-profile clients to help them promote their identities and corporate businesses. Anne has also taught adult business classes at numerous colleges. She's a company director, happily married, and a proud mother.

Today, after some time out of the workforce to care for her own family, including her parents, Anne decided to utilize her background as a communications professional to help bring about awareness of and change in a particular problem area that affects many millions of elders. Once elders reach this stage of their lives, they may not have the capacity or the energy to speak up themselves, as they once did.

She realized her skills could be put to good use; her expertise as a promotional business consultant for many years gave her a good grounding for helping to highlight the need to preserve an area of concern with a quickly growing population. She also recognized that as our aging population grows, so will the need to be even more diligent and vigilant in the area of senior and elder wealth protection—more specifically, their finances, lifestyles, and basic rights. Anne's priority is to provide a hub for communication where people who are looking for guidelines or some basic yet essential information can visit for assistance and support and can be kept up to date with the latest news on the subject and its developments.

Anne is a person who believes in the benefits of personal development, and her work these days is about education and whole-wealth preservation. She believes more knowledge will ultimately bring about a better system to look after people in the later stages of their lives. For those people who have been adversely affected by the ultimate betrayal, they will be provided with some ideas to assist them in dealing with it.

She believes in treating people with dignity and respect. However, these days, because of her awareness of the abuse of elders, she prefers to avoid people who are not of good character. She's determined to have a good life, and she enjoys running businesses. In addition to her public relations studies, she has also studied interior design, personal nutrition, and fitness. She loves her family's rural property, and her interests are in well-being, design and property styling, the outdoors, traveling, and being in the company of good friends and decent people.

Anne is an advocate for the elderly. She firmly believes that when people reach their later years, they have a lot to offer; they often have a wonderful sense of humor and much wisdom. Elders are an absolute pleasure to be in the company of, and they should be revered. She is also of the strong opinion that elder seniors have not only certain needs but rights and that they should be able to live their later years in the knowledge of that, feeling safe, comfortable, and secure.

ABOUT PROTECTING SENIORS WEALTH AND THE BENEFIT OF TRAINING WORKSHOPS

Anne first established a website late in 2014 as a vehicle to create more awareness after she was compelled to investigate the issue of elder financial abuse. Over a period of five years, she held conversations with many people who are regularly exposed to this in their chosen professions, and she listened to the many stories of those affected firsthand. Anne soon came to the realization that elder financial abuse is much more widespread than society knows. After listening to all the stories, she also heard about how it can be very difficult to try to work out what to do when a loved one becomes a victim of the ultimate betrayal.

In order to effectively provide a place for people to promptly locate helpful and practical information, a number of useful tools have been created. The site is for people in general, lawyers, accountants, bankers, financial advisors, aged care facilities, support services and their clients to access and receive a range of reference ideas, guidelines and material, professional help, and support. The website was established to manage a constantly increasing volume of communication. The website contains a listing of competent firms, along with media and news pages. If people care to subscribe, they can be kept up to date on latest changes. Professionals can refer their clients to the website and feel comfortable recommending it to their clients.

- Training Workshops
  Our comprehensive workshops are designed for firms, companies and organizations to assist their management and employees effectively deal with wealth abuse situations and protect their clients. Produced for people who work on the front lines, the classes provide all the additional awareness information in a professional environment to improve the level of customer service relating to financial abuse situations.

  Speaking Presentations
  Key note speaking at seminars or events provide an effective way to educate and inform large groups of employees, managers, members or clients, of the need for setting boundaries relating to prevention of financial senior exploitation. We actively encourage and speak at events.

- Consulting
  In-house consulting and training can be organized by arrangement for organizations who may be looking to provide a well-informed way to implement systems, train their people, and they can offer an effective service to their clients.

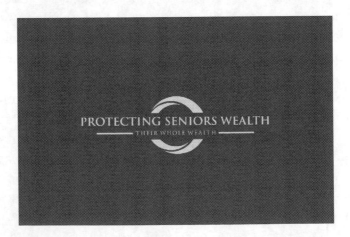

OTHER BOOK

The *Protecting Seniors' Wealth Guide* is an e-book or book featured on the website, along with this concept book. It's very informative and interesting, and it's a helpful, practical guide for people, assisting them to plan for protecting people in their later years. It can be a very useful tool to effectively help them to step in if there's a concern about financial abuse.

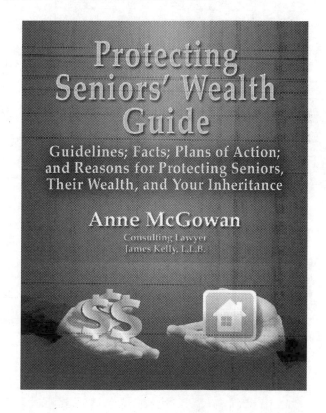

127

Parkinson's Disease

Parkinson's disease is a progressively degenerative neurological disorder that affects the control of body movements. If anyone wishes to donate for research or find out more information, there are organizations that help. They and their contact details are easily found via Google.

REFERENCES FOR THIS BOOK

www.legaldictionary.com

- *West's Encyclopedia of American Law*

- Australian Human Rights Commission
  www.humanrights.gov.au -- Refer to: Your Rights at Retirement
     5 Your Rights to be free of Financial Abuse
     5.1 Financial Abuse by family and friends

- Investor Protection Trust
  www.investorprotection.org—Go to the "Protect Yourself" page and click on "Elder Investment Fraud Video." The video title is "Elder Investment Fraud: A National Epidemic."

- State Trustees in Victoria Australia
  www.statetrustees.com.au -- Refer to *Protecting Elders Assets Study (PEAS): Ethical Management of Older Persons' Financial Assets (2009-2011)*

- - Actor Mickey Rooney speaks out against elder abuse before a Senate Committee on Aging - - Refer to Google and search for his story of abuse

- ABC News (Australian Broadcasting Corporation) –

http://www.abc.net.au/news/2016-05-02/calls-double
-to-elder-abuse-helpline-advocare/7375068

- Protecting Seniors Wealth shares media coverage, statistics, research,
  Cases, reports -- https://www.facebook.com/ protectingseniorswealth

- Investor Protection Trust (IPT)
  www.investorprotection.org -- Results of the IPT Elder Fraud and Financial Exploitation Survey: Nearly 1 in 5 U.S. Seniors Hit by Financial Swindles (2016)

FOR ADDITIONAL INFORMATION

- www.protectingseniorswealth.com.au

- Protecting Seniors Wealth Guide – Author is Anne McGowan, available on www.protectingseniorswealth.com.au, Amazon or Kindle

- National Committee to Prevent Elder Abuse (NCPEA) www.preventelderabuse.org—Go to the "Elder Abuse" page and click on "Financial Abuse" for a description.

- National Center on Elder Abuse (NCEA) www.ncea.aoa.gov—Go to the research brief "Abuse of Adults with a Disability," particularly the paragraph "What Does the Research Say?"

- COTA Australia www.cota.org.au -- Refer to National Elder Abuse Conference

- Elder Abuse Helpline Services available in Australia:
  * Australian Capital Territory -
    ACT Disability, Aged Carer Advocacy Service (ADACAS)
  * New South Wales - Seniors Rights Service Elder Abuse Helpline
  * South Australia – Aged Rights Advocacy Service (ARAS)
  * Queensland – Elder Abuse Prevention Unit (EAPU)
  * Tasmania – Advocacy Tasmania

* Victoria – Seniors Rights Victoria
* Western Australia - Advocare Incorporated

- www.elderabuseawarenessday.org.au

- International Network for the Prevention of Elder Abuse (INPEA) – http://www.inpea.net/home.html

- Parliament of Australia – Inquiry Into Older People and the Law (2007) - - Refer to Google to search for recommendations

- Victorian Government Inquiry Into Powers of Attorney (2010)

- Elder Law in Australia (second edition)
  Rodney Lewis is the author of this legal text

Printed in the United States
By Bookmasters